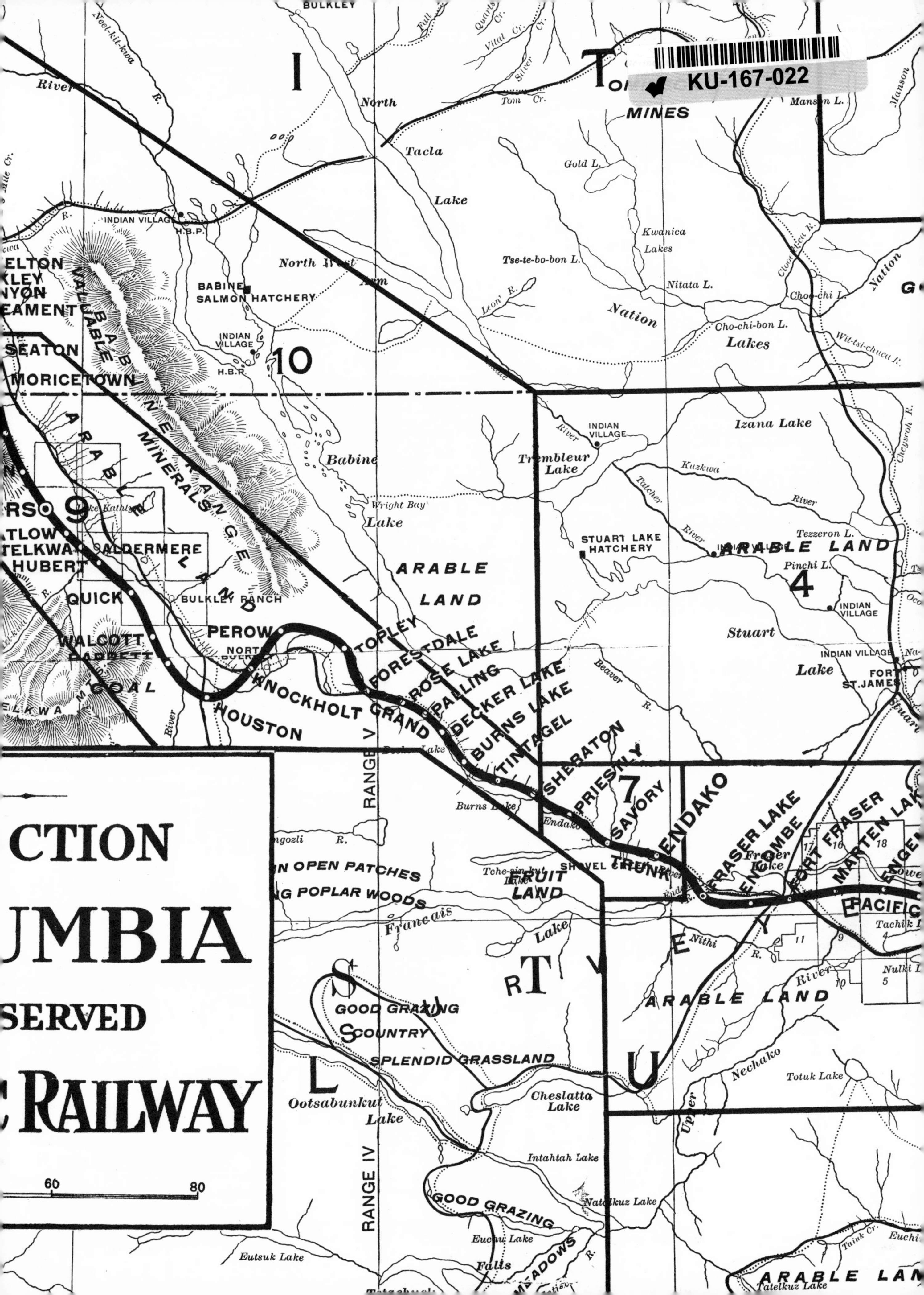
CTION
UMBIA
SERVED
C RAILWAY
BULKLEY
BABINE SALMON HATCHERY
INDIAN VILLAGE
H.B.P.
North West Arm
Babine Lake
Tacla Lake
MINES
Nation Lakes
Izana Lake
Trembleur Lake
STUART LAKE HATCHERY
ARABLE LAND
Stuart Lake
FORT ST. JAMES
SEATON
MORICETOWN
BABINE RANGE
VALUABLE MINERALS
ARABLE LAND
ALDERMERE
TELKWA
HUBERT
QUICK
BULKLEY RANCH
WALCOTT
PEROW
COAL
HOUSTON
KNOCKHOLT
TOPLEY
FORESTDALE
ROSE LAKE
GRAND
PALLING
DECKER LAKE
BURNS LAKE
TINTAGEL
SHERATON
PRIESTLY
SAVORY
ENDAKO
FRASER LAKE
ENCOMBE
FORT FRASER
MARTEN LAKE
PACIFIC
Burns Lake
Francais Lake
FRUIT LAND
GOOD GRAZING COUNTRY
SPLENDID GRASSLAND
Cheslatta Lake
Ootsabunkut Lake
Intahtah Lake
GOOD GRAZING
Natalkuz Lake
Eucha Lake
MEADOWS
Eutsuk Lake
Nechako
Totuk Lake
ARABLE LAND
Tatelkuz Lake
RANGE V
RANGE IV
60
80

SMITHERS

From Swamp to Village

by

R. Lynn Shervill

Canadian Cataloguing in Publication Data

Shervill, R. Lynn (Robert Lynn), 1946-
Smithers, from swamp to village

ISBN 0-9690737-0-4

1. Smithers (B.C.) - History. 2. Bulkley Valley (B.C.) - History. I. Smithers (B.C.) II. Title.
FC3849.S58S49 971.1'2 C81-091175-2
F1089.5.S58S49

ISBN 0-9690737-0-4

Published by
The Town of Smithers
Box 879
Smithers, B.C.
V0J 2N0
Canada

First Printing 1981

Printed and Bound by
D.W. Friesen & Sons Ltd.
Cloverdale, B.C.

PRINTED IN CANADA

Smithers Anniversary Logo by Terry Kline

SMITHERS
From Swamp to Village
by
R. Lynn Shervill

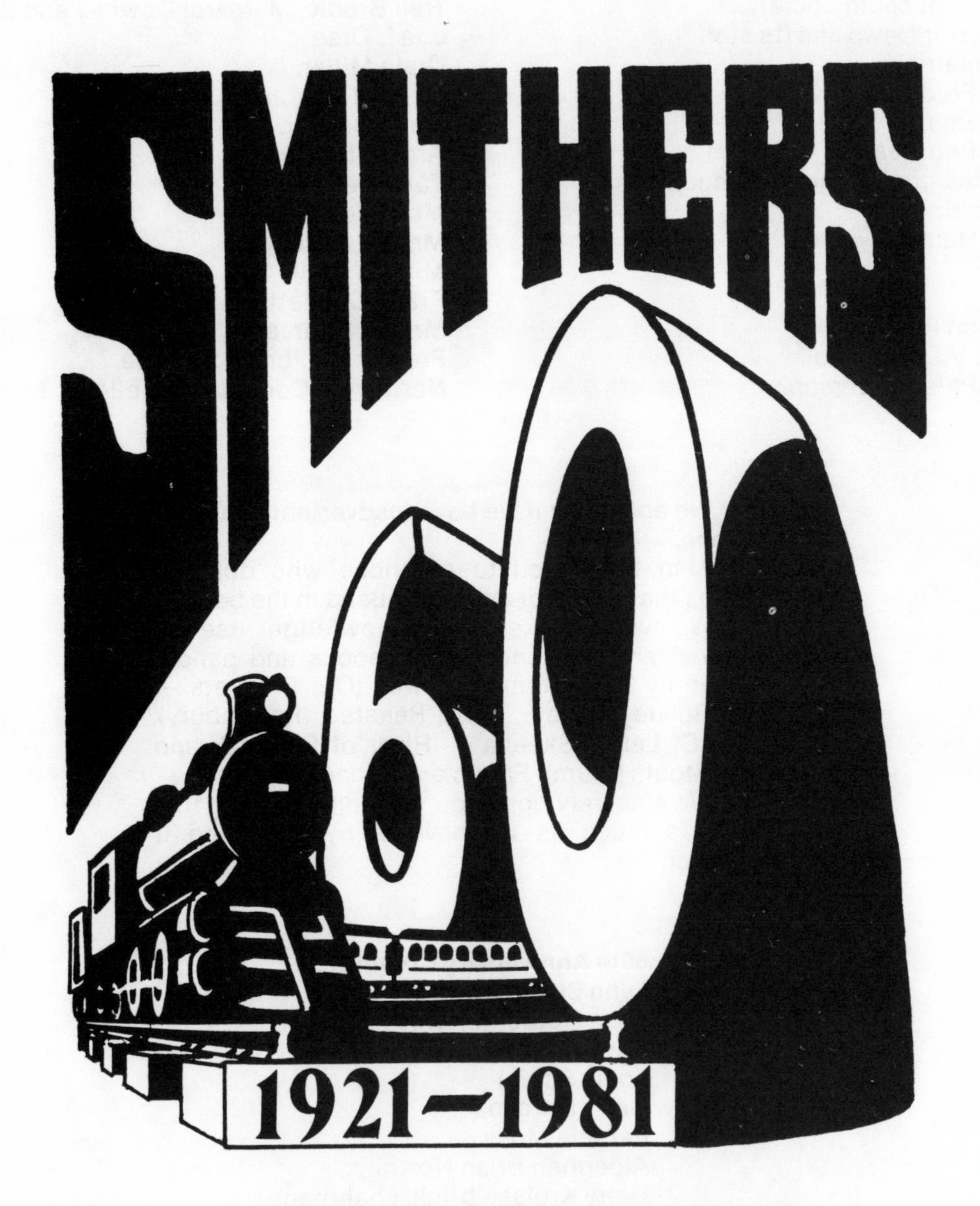

This book is the 60th Anniversary Project of the Town of Smithers

Logo by Terry Kline

ACKNOWLEDGEMENTS

This book is the result of the co-operative efforts of many people in the community.

The 60th Anniversary Committee would like to express its thanks to the Council of the Town of Smithers for sponsoring this project, and to the Town staff for their helpful assistance whenever it was needed.

We would also like to thank the following people who lent photographs and historical documents; who helped to identify people on old pictures; who did art work and generally assisted in producing this book:

Bulkley Valley Museum Society.
Smithers Interior News and its staff.
Mrs. Jean Kilpatrick.
Mr. and Mrs. Fred Riffel.
Gordon Williams.
Mr. and Mrs. Reg Heal.
Terry Kline (designer of the 1981 logo).
Mike Wakefield.
Mr. and Mrs. Harry Haywood.
Chris Dahlie.
Ken Warner.
The Ernie Hann Family.
Bob Evans, B.V.D. Hospital.
Mr. and Mrs. Peter Anderson.
Ralph Dieter.
Neil Brodie, Margaret Downey and Bunny Fink.
Joe L'Orsa.
Craig Millar.
Mr. and Mrs. Jack Green.
Harry Bakker.
Arnold DeEllion.
Tat Aida.
Mrs. Olga Evans.
Mrs. H. J. Kelly.
Mike O'Neill.
Frank Cuglietta.
Mrs. R. Buursema.
Provincial Library, Victoria.
Northwest Community College, Terrace.

We apologize if we have inadvertently missed anyone.

Also thank you to all those who donated photos that were not able to be used in the book.

We would like to acknowledge use of material and references from books and papers written by John Tupper Saywell (Our Pioneers — The Bulkley Valley), Terry Reksten (Rattenbury), Dr. R.G. Large (Skeena — River of Destiny), and Jack Mould (Stump Farms and Broadaxes).

We sincerely hope you will enjoy reading this book as much as we have enjoyed putting it together.

60th Anniversary Committee.
Lynn Shervill, author.
Tona Hetherington.
Oswald Hoskins.
Louis Schibli.
Gerry Brinkman.
Patricia Moss.
Alderman Brian Northup.
Harry Kruisselbrink, chairman.

TABLE OF CONTENTS

Front Inside Cover — Part of the Map of The Central Section of British Columbia. Grand Trunk Pacific Railway. 1911.

Back Inside Cover — Part of the Map of the Northern Interior of British Columbia. Father A.G. Morice, O.M.I. 1907.

Sir Alfred Waldron Smithers

The man in whose honor the Town of Smithers is named was born on October 4, 1850, the son of William Henry Smithers, a prominent official with the Bank of England. The paternal influence must have affected young Alfred strongly as he joined the London Stock Exchange at the age of 23 and further established himself in the world of finance as a partner in the firm of Ackroyd and Smithers.

He began his association with the Grand Trunk Railway in 1896 when, as director, he made his first trip to Canada. In 1909 he took over as chairman of the line, visiting this area occasionally in the company of Charles M. Hays, the G.T.P.'s general manager. Smithers retained his position as chairman until the G.T.P. was taken over by the Government of Canada several years later.

Little in the way of anecdotal material is available on Sir Alfred but Wiggs O'Neill, who worked along the route of the railway during Smithers' term as chairman, provided one light-hearted description of the man in an article entitled "Smithers and the Railway Era of Central B.C."

> "..... Sir Alfred (was) standing on the bank, well clear of the river; one steward would bait the hook, another would make the cast, and then they would bow and hand the rod to Sir Alfred and say 'Good fishing, m'Lord."

Entering politics in 1918, he represented the riding of Chislehurst in the British House of Commons for the next four years, being knighted in 1919. He died in 1924 at the age of 74.

The name of Knockholt, Sir Alfred's family home in Kent, England, now dignifies a small railway stop just east of Houston, B.C. and Lake Kathlyn, just west of Smithers, was named after one of Sir Alfred's daughters. Alfred Avenue, in downtown Smithers, is named after Sir Alfred himself.

Indian Village and smoke houses.

INTRODUCTION

Initially, the Bulkley Valley gave its all, in terms of spiritual and physical sustenance, to the Carrier Indians. The lands around Smithers were their hunting grounds and transportation corridors. This period of history, sometimes oddly called the pre-history of the area, is dealt with in a number of publications. The most accessible nowadays are Father Morice's History of The Northern Interior of British Columbia, The Downfall of Temlaham (Hazelton) by Marius Barbeau and a new book entitled Proud Past, a history of Moricetown written by Maureen and Frank Cassidy.

In the preparation of this book on Smithers' history, it became immediately evident that even though the valley continues to nurture the Carriers today, they have suffered mightily since the arrival of the white man. The history of the relationship between the races, when and if it is written, will not be something which the white man can look to with pride, as even a cursory examination of early newspapers will demonstrate.

It is not, however, our intention to deal with that relationship here. When this publication was initially proposed we envisioned it as a chronicle of Smithers from 1921, the date of its incorporation as a village, to the present. However, almost from the first day of the research effort, it became ever more clear that the crucial

An Indian medicine man in full regalia.

aspects of the community's founding and the patterns and traditions of its development began well prior to 1921 and were essentially complete 30 years ago. That is not to say events since 1950 have been inconsequential. Rather they represent a certain maturing process made possible by the preparatory events of preceding decades. And it is with these events, and the people behind them, that this publication concerns itself. The orientation has been chronological and the admittedly incomplete selection of material governed primarily by its significance in the development of the area and secondly by its human interest value.

R. Lynn Shervill

Mr. and Mrs. David Dennis of Moricetown in ceremonial dress.

CHAPTER ONE

The Telegraph Trail

The first major incursion by the white man into what the Indians called the Watsonquah (River) Valley came with an attempt to construct an overland telegraph line connecting North America and the European and Asian continents via Russia. All attempts to link the old and new worlds by means of a submarine cable across the Atlantic, the latest being in 1858, had failed. The overland route was the brainchild of Perry McDonough Collins, a California gold rush veteran who later obtained a posting as commercial agent for the United States government in Russia. Encouraged by the failure of the submarine cable, Collins approached the U.S. Government, the Western Union Telegraph Company and his Russian friends with his proposal. The line would run from San Francisco to the British American Boundary and then north through uncharted wilderness to cross the Bering Sea. The Russian Government was to construct the line connecting with the European telegraph system.

By 1863 the Russians were already working on their portion of the line. The Western Union Telegraph Company endorsed Collins' plan in 1864, expecting to spend about $1.5 million to span the 5,000 miles with the talking wire. Col. Charles S. Bulkley, who had been a communications expert with the Union Army during the American civil war, was named engineer-in-chief for the entire project.

According to historian John Tupper Saywell, the line followed the old Cariboo Road and had been constructed as far as Quesnel by the beginning of 1866. The actual trail had been blazed as far as Fraser Lake. From there the line was to turn north towards Stuart Lake and then into Takla country, but Edward Conway, one of Col. Bulkley's assistants, determined that a more westerly route was the better plan. In June, 1866, he sent an exploration team into the Bulkley Valley. What they found was recorded by Thomas Elwyn, a magistrate who had joined the construction crew to resolve both internal disputes and those which might arise between the crew and area native people.

> "A most favourable report has been received of the country between this (Fraser Lake) and Rocher de Boule (Hazelton): a valley having plenty of grass and very little timber runs up the whole distance. The Telegraph Company (is) making an excellent trail for pack animals along this line; the timber is cleared to a width from twelve to sixteen feet and all small streams have been bridged."

The line entered the valley near the source of the Bulkley, crossed the river several times and then took to the heights on the river's east side all the way to Moricetown. It is possible, even today, to find sections of the road used by the construction crews in the Driftwood area. At McClure (Tyee) Lake (named after a surveyor with the telegraph crew) Magistrate Elwyn again recorded his impressions of the country.

Original telegraph cabin at Tyee Lake in 1910. It was located on the present Camp Caledonia site. Hank Boss was the telegraph operator in 1910.

"... there is a stretch of country more favourable for settlement than any other part of the colony. With the exception of a few heavy patches of scattered timber, the land is either entirely open or covered with small timber brush; grass and peavine grow to the height of from three to five feet..... berries of many kinds grow in greater abundance throughout this section than in any other part of the country which I have visited."

Elwyn later reported that the land between McClure Lake and Moricetown could support "probably nearly all the crops grown in the north of England." He also suggested the mountains bordering the area might one day support an extensive mining industry. From Moricetown the line continued west, crossing the Bulkley again at Hagwilget and north to Telegraph Creek on the Stikine.

However, in 1866, yet another attempt was being made to lay a submarine cable across the Atlantic. On July 27, a steamship carrying one end of that cable arrived off the shores of Newfoundland. The other end of the cable was in Ireland. Locally, work continued on the overland line until October, in the hope the submarine cable would ultimately fail, and was then abandoned.

"Collins, Bulkley... and many others had lost the 'battle of time'," wrote Saywell, "but during this struggle the Bulkley Valley had become a part of written history due to its strategic location on the advancing front of the overland route."

For the next 25 years, the telegraph trail through the Bulkley Valley was used by the occasional pack train headed north but little, if any, real exploration of the area was conducted until 1892 when A.L. Poudrier surveyed the area for the provincial government. After arriving in Hazelton by steamer, Poudrier's party built a wagon road from that point to Moricetown and then proceeded to survey nine townships. Poudrier, as had Magistrate Elwyn, did not fail to

The Barrett Ranch at Barrett Lake, B.C. It was one of the early ranches in the valley.

The Sealy Ranch in Driftwood. Started by J.C.K. Sealy, it was until recently owned by Bill Morris.

notice the mineral, forestry and agricultural potential of the valley. He made note of the coal outcroppings in the Telkwa Valley. In recommending a road be built into the area for settlement purposes, Poudrier stated:

> "The value of the Bulkley Valley, besides its good land and grazing, lies in the fact that when the time comes for the American people to build a road . . . to Alaska, this valley offers the best route."

With neither immediate financial or political benefit to be realized, the provincial government did not jump at Poudrier's suggestion for a road. But the potential of the valley was no longer going unnoticed. The telegraph line, now known as the Dominion Telegraph, was being extended into the Yukon which necessitated regular maintenance of that portion of the line already constructed. Supplies were delivered by pack train from a government ranch on the east side of the Bulkley, facing the mouth of the Morice, to the construction parties and numerous line cabins. The pack train was owned by Ed Charleson, son of a telegraph construction superintendent, Charles Barrett and J.C.K. Sealy. Barrett, after whom Barrett Station is named, later bought the ranch, renamed it the Diamond D. and lived there until his death in 1946. Jack Sealy later divided his time between a hotel in Hazelton, a butcher shop in Smithers and one of the very early and successful ranches in Driftwood. Driftwood was also the site of the Hudson's Bay Company ranch, established in 1898 on Driftwood Creek near what is now the Nageli farm. Used primarily to winter company horses, the ranch was also the site of early agricultural experimentation in the valley. Results of this work were later used to draw settlers into the area. Now used by pack trains and fur traders, the valley also provided a convenient transportation corridor for another breed of pioneer, prospectors bound for the Klondike gold rush in the Yukon. While most Klondikers travelled north via steamer from west coast ports, many of those who could not afford the expensive passage walked. Thus, between 1897 and 1901, the old telegraph trail through the Bulkley Valley served as an important access route to the northern gold fields. Some of those hopeful prospectors later returned to the valley, having already noted its mineral potential.

Formal attempts to bring large numbers of settlers to the Bulkley area were initiated as early as 1902 by men, who like Elwyn and Poudrier, had been favourably impressed with the natural richness of this particular valley. At one point, early in 1902, a southern newspaper reported there were actually 100 Vancouver-based families planning to make the trek north. This venture, and a number of other settlement schemes, never materialized, not because the valley fell short of its reported potential, but on account of its isolation. As one visitor put it: "Not withstanding the country's natural advantages, I consider it would be practically impossible for a

Government road camp near Lake Kathlyn.

man to profitably engage in either farming or stock raising until some better means of communication is established than at present."

Perhaps the most controversial of the early settlement schemes was one established by the B.C. Government to assist some of the 8,000 Canadian Boer War veterans to re-locate in their homeland. Each volunteer would be offered 160 acres of land free of charge. While some of these men actually did move onto the land, others sold their "scrips" to speculators. Of the approximately 100 applications made for Bulkley Valley land, more than half were, over a period of time, acquired by speculators.

One of these speculators was Francis Mawson Rattenbury, one of B.C.'s most controversial and best-known architects, and a man who promoted the valley throughout North America and Europe, albeit out of pure self-interest.

Rattenbury, having already designed and supervised the construction of the Parliament Buildings and the Empress Hotel in Victoria, turned his attention to another venture in 1902. It was in that year that Canada's oldest railway, the Grand Trunk, announced its intention to construct a transcontinental railway from Moncton, N.B. to the Pacific. The line east of Winnipeg was to be the responsibility of the Federal government. The western section would be built by the Grand Trunk. The central B.C. portion was to run along the Nechako and Bulkley Rivers with a west coast terminus on Kaien Island at the mouth of the Skeena. Shortly after the announcement, in 1903, Rattenbury purchased 11,000 acres in the Nechako Valley and somewhere in the order of 50,000 acres in the Bulkley Valley, a large portion of it between Telkwa and Moricetown. He was to spend the next 20 years promoting that acreage, mostly through the Rattenbury Lands Company, to would-be settlers from Canada, the United States and Great Britain. The effects of Rattenbury's speculative efforts, both on himself and the valley, will be discussed later.

If the Grand Trunk Pacific Railway Company, as it was officially named in 1903, had had its way, the railroad would never have passed through what became Smithers, nor the already established community of Hazelton. The company's intention was to turn its line west at Telkwa, proceed up the Telkwa River, eventually linking with the Copper River, and then along the Skeena to its mouth, thereby shortening the line by fifty miles. The provincial government objected, claiming this route would leave the mineral and agriculture potential of a large portion of the valley undeveloped. The G.T.P. eventually agreed, having realized that north from Hazelton would be the most obvious route for a future branch line to the Dawson Creek area.

Construction on the western section of the line began in 1907 at Prince Rupert and had reached Hazelton by the winter of 1913. The first divisional point, of three to be established between the western terminus and Prince George,

Transportation was primitive before the arrival of the G.T.P. Here several dog sled teams travel along the G.T.P. right-of-way near the Skeena River.

was Pacific, between Hazelton and Terrace. There were two obvious sites for the second divisional point. The first was Hubert, located on a flat strip of land on the west side of the Bulkley River about 10 miles east of Telkwa. The second was just across the river from Telkwa where the Grand Trunk had already invested money in real estate and had leased coal properties. A third possibility was a location about seven miles west of Telkwa, but no one, except for a few settlers and speculators, had much confidence the railway would choose this site.

From the railway's point of view, Hubert would have been ideal. However speculators, anticipating location of the divisional point at Hubert, had bought up much of the land in hopes of profiting at the G.T.P.'s expense. It is not clear why the Aldermere-Telkwa site was ruled out, but it was on the wrong side of the river and, surprisingly enough, there was local opposition. A Board of Trade resolution passed in 1913 read as follows:

The G.T.P. passenger train chug-a-lugging its way past Lake Kathlyn.

G.T.P. Engine no. 102 in 1913, during railway construction.

> "Resolved, that the Board of Trade of Aldermere pledges itself to resist to the utmost the attempts on the part of the Grand Trunk Pacific to thrust a station down our throats with its accompanying horde of shacks and cons."

Given this situation, the railway, with much secrecy, turned its attention to a section of very swampy but flat land at the foot of Hudson Bay Mountain. As stated earlier, some of the required land at this site was already privately owned. What happened next has been recorded by Dr. R.G. Large in his book, *Skeena - River of Destiny.*

> ". . . the firm of Aldous and Murray (Telkwa) was engaged by the G.T.P. to acquire the necessary land. Strict secrecy was necessary and the report was allowed to circulate that Hubert had been chosen, and a party of

The first regular through passenger train arriving in Smithers on March 9th, 1914 — an historic occasion for the new community!

The G.T.P. roundhouse and water tower, circa 1917.

A G.T.P. engine getting a good servicing in the new Smithers roundhouse. The large pipe on the right was used to heat the work pits below the engines.

A passenger train standing by Smithers' temporary railway station, present site of the C.N.R. freightshed.

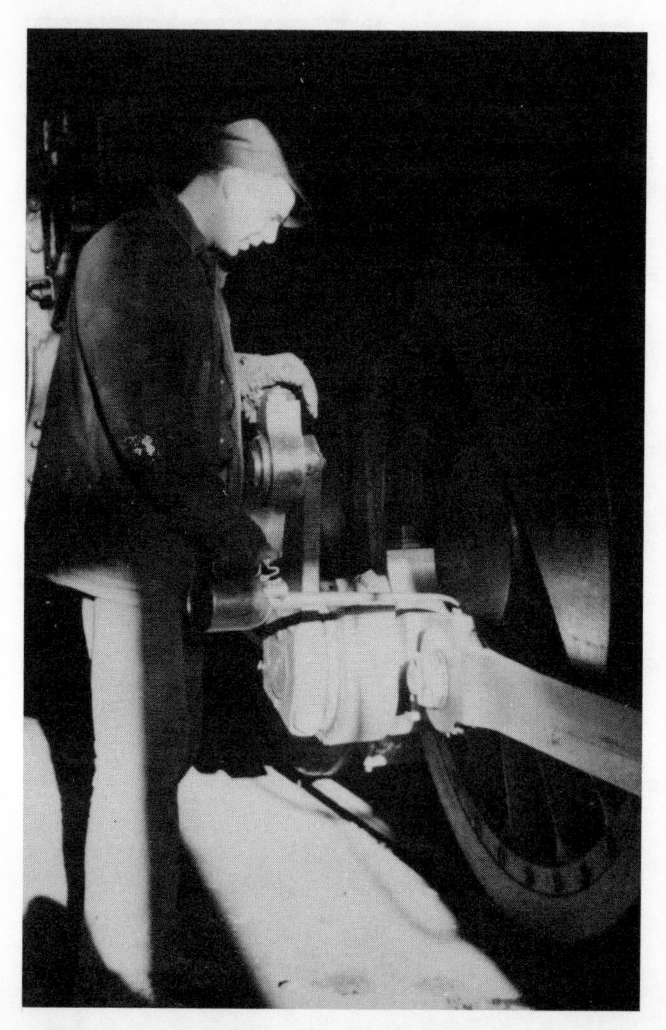

" 'Tis the squeaky wheel that getteth the grease," generously applied by roundhouse machinist Jack Green.

surveyors was sent in to lay out a town. In the meantime, Murray had his brother in Erie, Pennsylvania, write him a letter announcing that a company was interested in a settlement scheme in the Bulkley Valley and commissioned him to purchase land. This he proceeded to do, buying up all the farms in the chosen area at $50 an acre. As soon as the land was procured, the surveyors were withdrawn from Hubert and the new townsite of Smithers was announced."

In preparing a promotional brochure on the town in 1914, the year after they "acquired" the townsite for the G.T.P., Aldous and Murray told a slightly more respectable version of the story.

"The selection of the division point was of great importance and was not made lightly. Thorough exploration was first carried on and complete reports of engineers and traffic men examined. At last an almost level site on the south side of the Bulkley River, 226 miles east of Prince Rupert and 231 miles west of Prince George, in the very heart of the rich Bulkley Valley, was chosen. Some idea of the importance attached to this place by the Railway Company may be gained from the fact that it was named Smithers after its highest official, Mr. Alfred Waldron Smithers, Chairman of its Board of Directors.

Temporary Railway Station, Smithers.

January 13-14

G.U.Ryley Esq

Grand Trunk Pacific Development Co Ltd

Winnipeg

Dear Sir;-

The following is a resolution passed by the Citizens Assoc of Smithers, at a special meeting held on January 12th for the purpose of drafting this letter;-

We beg to direct your attention to the immediate requirments regarding local improvments in Smithers.

At the present time there is no feasible roadway to the freight yards, the road being impassible, this same condition exists on Main St where the earth which has been taken from the ditches on the west side is eighteen inches higher, than the level of the ground on the east side, this will cause a good deal of dis-satisfaction in the spring, as the surface water will have no chance of getting away.

The slabs which were placed on Main St by your company, late in the fall of 1913, are of very little use, as they sink deep in to the mud, and not being uniform, the higher ones slide ahead of the wheels of the heavy loaded wagons. We consider the slabbing of Main St as being of no use whatever, as it can not be made a satisfactory traffic road.

We also wish to direct your attention to Alfred Street, which is absolutely impassible during soft weather. The property holders of this street have gone to the personal expense of having the stumps removed.

The only satisfactory way to place the streets in a proper condition is to ditch both sides of the streets, in order to give them proper drainage (these ditches need not be deep), crossway with timber turnpike on top of this, put a crown finish on the hump, then finish with gravel.

We beg to direct your attention to the fact that the fiscal townsite agents directed that all livery stables and blacksmith shops be located between Columbia and Manitoba Streets on 3rd Ave, several of these places have been established, and as yet 3rd Ave has not even been cleared to their places of business.

The ditches which were completed on Main St and 2nd are in a serious condition, having sluffed in, in several places stopping the natural flow of water, and every indication points to more trouble in this respect in the spring.

The earth from the ditch on 2nd Ave was not properly leveled off, making it impassible for vehicles, several loaded wagons having capsized.

At present, the main wagon road has not been completed in to Smithers, between 5th and 8th Ave being a swamp.

Some immediate action should be taken, regarding the installation of a sewage system, water system and a electric lighting plant.

The sanitary conditions of the town are none too favourable and and unless immediate xxxxxxxxxx financially percautions are taken, we may have considerable sickness of a serious nature in the spring.

The town needs immediate assistance financially from the townsite Company, and we trust you will lose no time in support of the requirments mentioned.

We, as the representatives of the people of Smithers must ask you for a reply at once, as the future of this town depends entirely on what you will do this spring.

Yours truly

Smithers Citizens Assoc

per--------------------------

Secretary

Some of the problems the Citizens Association had to deal with. These problems amply bear out Dr. Large's reservations about the suitability of the new townsite.

"The Bulkley Valley is a section of wonderful natural wealth. It is one of the largest agricultural areas of British Columbia. Vast mineral deposits and valuable forests surround it. Its streams, that have run idly to the sea since the dawn of creation, will supply inexhaustible water-power. They are waiting to do their part in the development that is to come.

"From every standpoint the location of Smithers was a happy one. It combined all the essentials, a wide tributary country with great resources, easily accessible to the railway centre. Its site for town-building and the installation of division point facilities is ideal and there is plenty of room for the expansion of the future city that will be necessary in later years. The railway's wise choice of its division point shows that its chief consideration was to provide for the development of the country through which it passes and the ready collection and distribution of traffic."

As Dr. Large later stated, the only thing to commend this particular location was its flatness. "The townsite itself was a swamp ..... Although the land was drained, the subsoil was composed of layers of quicksand and clay and foundations could only be laid by driving piling - in some cases one pile on top of another." As testimony to this it might be noted that the Smithers post office rests on two sets of piles, each set 60 feet in length.

While the future of Smithers was now more or less guaranteed by the railway, the once rapid growth of Telkwa and area had slowed considerably. Perhaps the major blow to the village was a fire that destroyed most of its commercial section and a pattern of rapid growth that had started at the turn of the century. Historically, the area's first official settler, according to the 1900 voters list, was Gabriel Lacroix, with a small farm on the east side of the Bulkley south of what was to become the village. The first family to arrive was that of Fred Heal who took up his pre-emption on the east side of Tyee Lake in 1903. By 1906 they had been joined by several others, including Joe Bourgon, Lem Broughton, William Croteau, Joe Coyle, Frank Dockrill, Harry Fink, Jack McNeil, and Rev. F.L. Stephenson. Some of these settlers listed the community of Aldermere as their home.

The original Aldermere townsite, located on the ridge above what is now Telkwa, was staked in 1904 by John Dorsey, an agent with the North Coast Land Company. By 1905, the site had been surveyed, land purchased and buildings erected. By 1907 the townsite of Telkwa had been surveyed and a hotel and church were under construction. According to historian Saywell there were at least three reasons for the almost simultaneous emergence of Telkwa so close to Aldermere.

"Aldermere had no water supply; lots were far

Gabriel LaCroix's farm across the river from the original Hubert townsite. LaCroix was the area's first official settler.

cheaper in Telkwa for speculators had not got hold of the townsite and, more important, if the railway did come through, Telkwa, not Aldermere, was the logical site of the station."

Confidence in the longevity of any new community was often demonstrated by the emergence of a local newspaper. In Telkwa, this occurred about 1906 with publication of The Bulkley Pioneer. Published originally in Vancouver by the North Coast Land Company, The Pioneer was moved closer to its subject material by company agent Dorsey who hired one Joe Coyle as editor. Coyle put out his first issue in August of 1907 by which time Telkwa was boasting a laundry and bakery, two hotels, a real estate office, run by R.L. Gale, and a ferry company operated by George Duhamel and Tom Gague. The population, however, was still not sufficient to support a newspaper and in 1908 Joe Coyle left for Hazelton where he began publication of the Omineca Herald. Coyle returned about three years later, starting another newspaper which he named The Interior News. In his absence Telkwa had become a major centre in the Bulkley Valley, as reported by historian Saywell.

"By 1912 the business sections of Telkwa and Aldermere, largely the former, had been considerably extended; rooms had been added to all the hotels; there were now four general stores, owned by F.L. Charleson, R.S. Sargent, L.J. McArthur and Louis Schorn; J. Mason Adams had built a drug store and the Union Bank had established a branch. In addition, there were several restaurants, Kennedy's pool room and cigar store, a barber shop, newstand, lumber yard, harness shop, rooming house, livery stable and a sash and door factory."

All of this, however, was lost on the night of April 13, 1914. A fire, which started in the rear of Kennedy's pool room, levelled most buildings on either side of the street. While the rebuilding started almost immediately, a number of the local businessmen, who were already expanding their operations into Smithers, decided not to reconstruct in Telkwa. These men soon formed the core of an extremely active and growth-minded group that would guide the development of Smithers for the next two decades.

The Telkwa fire occurred just six days after the first through train steamed into and out of its central divisional point at Smithers. The new

The Fred Heal family was the first family to move into the area, arriving in 1903. Here Fred's grandson, Reg Heal, is plowing on his father Ernie's ranch.

A horse drawn work sled in front of Broughton and McNeil's store at Lake Kathlyn.

community, still referred to as Squatterville by some, because of its large number of tents, was taking shape quickly. A newspaper report from October of 1913, just a few months before the rail service began, provides a comprehensive portrait of the new town.

"Although the town is only a few months old,

Several freighting outfits passing through Aldermere in 1913. The middle outfit belongs to Jack Beaton, a well-known name in early days.

Telkwa in 1915.

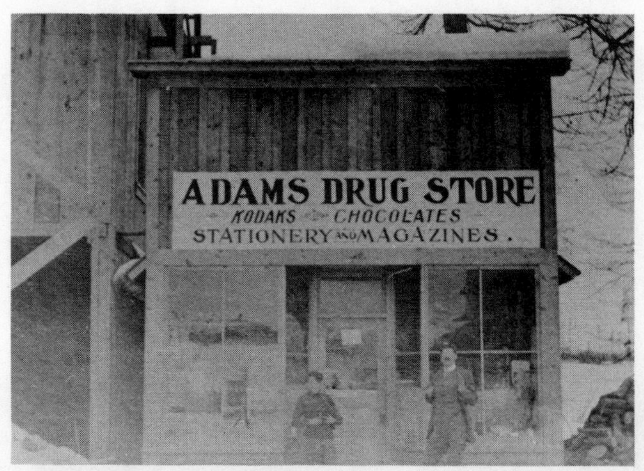

Adams Drug Store in Telkwa.

Clearing the Smithers townsite.

there has been a large number of businesses started here, as fast as buildings can be put up others are to be established. On Alfred Street two pool rooms have been opened up. One of these is conducted by H.P. Jones and . . . the other by H.W. Kraus.

"In between the pool rooms is the Smithers Rooming House run by James Girling, who is gaining quite a reputation with the travelling public. His building is not completed yet, but he had installed a large number of beds and is doing quite a business.

"Henry and Dunlop, the new real estate firm, is putting up a building on Murphy Street, just opposite Girling's rooming house, and they expect to have their quarters ready for occupancy within a couple of weeks. Both members of the firm are well known in the district and it is almost a certainty that they will do well from the start. On the corner of Alfred and Main the work of excavating for Mr. Bigelow's new building is under way, and when completed a business will be started similar to that which is conducted in Telkwa by Mr. Bigelow.

Wiggs O'Neill takes area residents on a trip from Hazelton to Telkwa and back — a fine way to spend a holiday. The vehicle was a Packard truck, used by O'Neill as a taxi and general transport in the early 1900's.

"On the opposite side of Main Street is Frizzell's Meat Market. Mr. Frizzell was one of the first to see the opportunity offered here for his line of business and lost no time in getting established. He ships in meat of all kinds from Prince Rupert twice a week and always has a fresh supply of fish, oysters, etc. on hand. Adjoining the meat market is the Smithers Sign Works, conducted by G.L. Hawkins. In a large tent on Alfred Avenue, between Main and Queen is the Oyster Bay Cafe, conducted by Victor Catway, who formerly ran a restaurant in New Hazelton. Although doing business in a tent Mr. Catway has it well arranged inside and the service is excellent.

"Just up the street a short distance is the Royal Cafe under the management of Robert Starr, who has been following construction for some time. He has now decided to stay here permanently and will later occupy the lower floor of Mr. Schuler's building on Alfred Avenue between Main and King. Occupying several lots at the corner of Alfred Avenue and Queen Street is the lumber yard and selling office of the Williams-Carr Lumber and Investment Company. Their building is nearly completed now and a crew of men are busy unloading shipments of lumber and other building material at the yards.

"Just across the street from the lumber yard is the sash and door factory of Smith and Eggleston, the well-known contracting firm . . . They are now building an office at the corner of Alfred Avenue and Queen Street. The firm handles all kinds of coast lumber, building materials of every description, and are selling agents for the Seymour Lake Lumber Co., whose mill is located just below the railway yards. This mill has a capacity of ten thousand feet per day and has been running steadily since last July.

"At Broadway and Queen is the Methodist church building, which is nearing completion. It will have an auditorium and lounging rooms at the rear where homeless men may spend their evenings. On Main Street, at the corner of Broadway, Lynch Bros. are building their new store . . . . . On Broadway between Main and King streets a two-story building has been erected by

A very early shot of Main Street showing some of the first construction. A number of the tents that earned Smithers the name of Squatterville are still up in this picture.

Smithers in the winter of 1913.

Smithers as it looked in 1914.

Three extremely well-groomed gentlemen enjoyed the view of Smithers from the hill.

Murdie and Smith, the upper floor of which is devoted to bedrooms, and as soon as the finishing work is done on the lower floor they will conduct a bakery and coffee house.

"Wilcocks and Wolseley's two new buildings on Main Street between Broadway and First are almost completed and their stock of general merchandise is already ordered. In the smaller of the two buildings they will conduct a real estate and insurance business. At First and Main is located Sargent's Smithers Store, which, together with the warehouse, entirely covers the corner lot. J.A. McDonald, who was formerly in charge of Sargent's Telkwa store, is manager. On the corner of Main and Second is located Adams' drug store and the post office. The business is being conducted at present in a tent, but as soon as his building is completed Mr. Adams will move his stock. Across the street from the drug store is being erected a building for the Union Bank of Canada. Between Second and Third on Main is located the Smithers Cafe, conducted by Stickney and Drummond. They are still doing business in a tent but expect to have their building ready soon. On the lot now occupied by the tent restaurant Sweeney and Orchard will put up a building for bowling alleys, which they already have on hand, and they will conduct a resort similar to the one run by them in Telkwa.

"At the corner of Main and Third is being built the new home of the Williams-Carr Lumber and Investment Co., townsite agents. On the opposite corner of Main and Third is Mr. Chisholms hardware store. Mr. Chisholm is doing business in a tent on the rear of his

Main Street as seen from the Railway Station . The corduroy that formed the base of the street is plainly visible.

Loading a pack horse (or "throwing a diamond hitch" as it was called) at Broughton and McNeil's store at Lake Kathlyn.

lot while waiting for his building to be finished. A.M. Tod is one of the latest arrivals in Smithers and lost no time in working up a business. He is a practical electrician and has secured a number of contracts for wiring buildings. John Wander, the barber, while not yet engaged in business, has his building nearly completed and his furnishings are now on their way from the coast. His shop will have two chairs and a couple of bathrooms in the rear.

"The livery men of Smithers and Telkwa have combined their forces this week and will continue their business under the name of the Bulkley Valley Transfer Co. The Smithers stables at Third and Columbia will be under the management of Mr. Beaton, while Brab Hoops and Wm. Henry will look after the Telkwa end. On Alfred Street between Main and King is located L. Schuler, an architect and builder who came here early last summer to take part in the building up of the town. He is erecting a large building on his lots for which he has already secured tenants. In a tent adjoining the Smithers Pool Room is McArthur's store. Mr. McArthur has been doing business in the district for several years and was the first to start a store in the new town. The Anglican church building, located at the corner of Broadway and King, will be ready to hold services early next month."

With that kind of growth pattern in mind, there was little skepticism about the future success of the town. Early in 1914, even before completion of the railroad, residents sported lapel buttons stating: "5,000 population by 1915." The outbreak of World War One later that year put an end to both the optimism and the rate of growth. By the end of the war in 1918, Smithers' population stood at 350 and by 1920, after extensive promotion of the area by both government and private land companies, the figure stood at only 700.

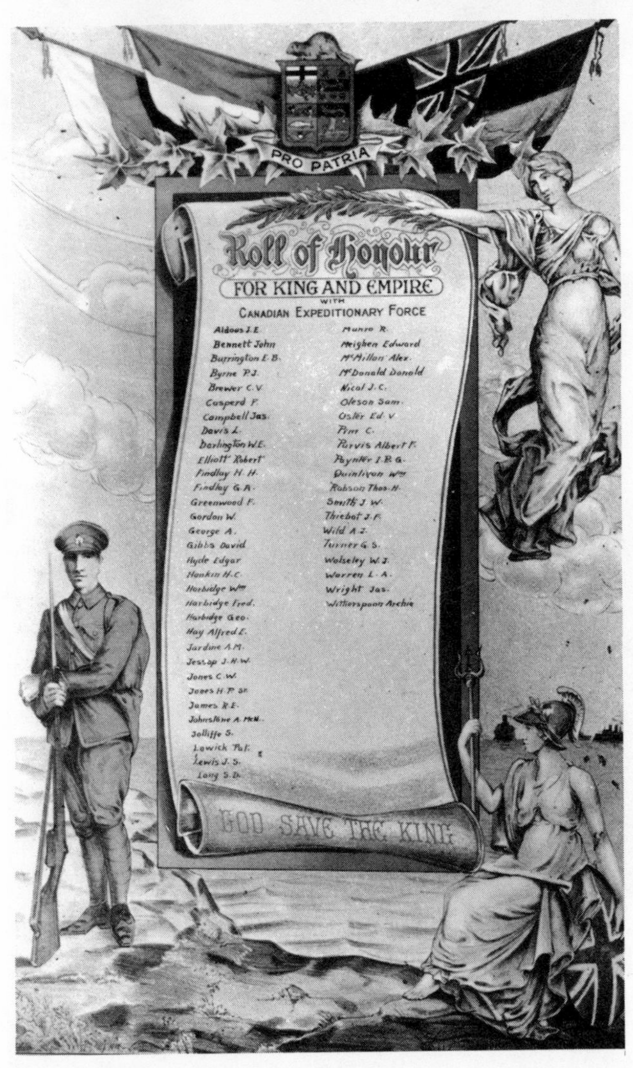

The opposing influences affecting the growth of Smithers. On one hand, the optimistic promotion of land sales as symbolized by the active Land Sales office. On the other hand, the outbreak of World War I.

Harvesting
Killam

CHAPTER 2

Ploughshares, Picks & Picaroons

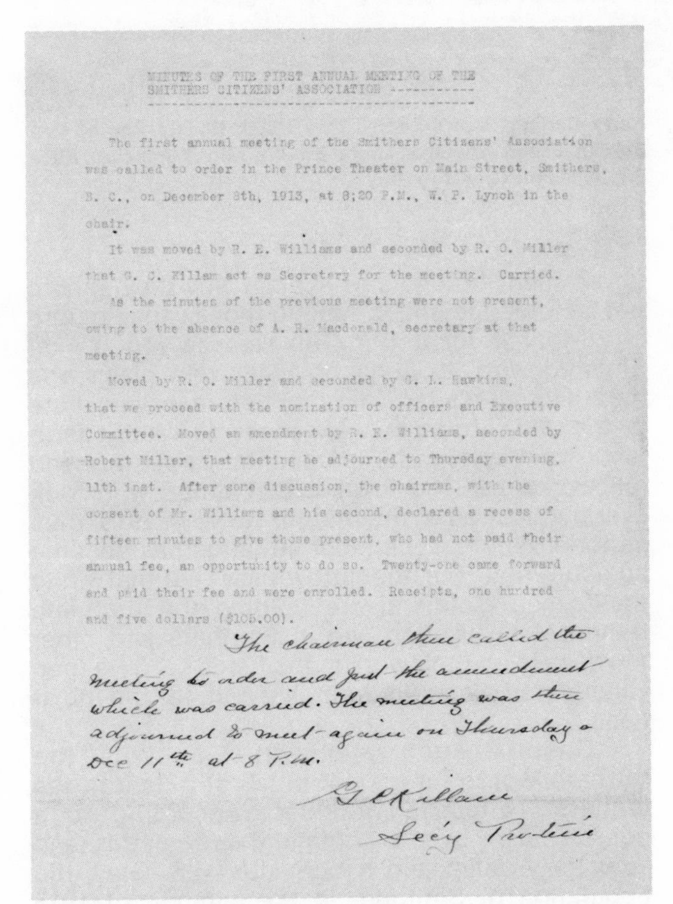

MINUTES OF THE FIRST ANNUAL MEETING OF THE SMITHERS CITIZENS' ASSOCIATION

The first annual meeting of the Smithers Citizens' Association was called to order in the Prince Theater on Main Street, Smithers, B. C., on December 8th, 1913, at 8;20 P.M., W. P. Lynch in the chair.

It was moved by R. E. Williams and seconded by R. O. Miller that G. C. Killam act as Secretary for the meeting. Carried.

As the minutes of the previous meeting were not present, owing to the absence of A. R. Macdonald, secretary at that meeting.

Moved by R. O. Miller and seconded by G. L. Hawkins, that we proceed with the nomination of officers and Executive Committee. Moved an amendment by R. E. Williams, seconded by Robert Miller, that meeting be adjourned to Thursday evening, 11th inst. After some discussion, the chairman, with the consent of Mr. Williams and his second, declared a recess of fifteen minutes to give those present, who had not paid their annual fee, an opportunity to do so. Twenty-one came forward and paid their fee and were enrolled. Receipts, one hundred and five dollars ($105.00).

The chairman then called the meeting to order and put the amendment which was carried. The meeting was then adjourned to meet again on Thursday Dec 11th at 8 P.M.

G C Killam
Secy Pro-tem

Minutes of the first Annual Meeting of the Citizens Association. It appears no earth shattering business was dealt with at this meeting.

Within 12 months of the railroad's completion, the new town had formed its first Citizens Association, an organization not dissimilar to a present day chamber of commerce though broader in scope. In addition to its prime function, inducing greater settlement and commerce in the area, the association addressed itself to such matters as cemetery regulation, fire protection, the state of the Main Street drainage ditch and, eventually, incorporation. G.C. Killam, many of whose pictures are included in this publication, was one of the founding members. During that same year the first school board was formed and the first school opened with 17 students registered under the tutelage of Miss M.K. Downey. The Church of England, the Roman Catholic Church and the Methodist Church all constructed houses of worship, an outdoor skating rink was built, and a bridge was being constructed across the Bulkley River at the foot of Main Street.

Joseph L. Coyle, former editor of The Bulkley Pioneer in Telkwa and The Omineca Herald in Hazelton, moved his paper, The Interior News, from Telkwa to Smithers. Through the pages of this weekly journal valley residents were, for the next four years, to follow events of the First World War which began in August of 1914. The beginning of the war put an abrupt end to speculative promises of rapid growth made on behalf of the town by G.T.P. agents Aldous and Murray. The future of the town, they had rashly

Miss Downey's class at the Methodist Church, 1914. The adults are (L-R): Mr. Karus, school trustee, Miss Mary Downey (later Mrs. Fred Watson) and Rev. C.E. Batzold, Methodist Minister. The students (not necessarily in order) are: Dora Bannister, Harry Darling, Frank Smith, Tom Heisi, Donald Smith, Mae Brooks, Eileen Wilcocks, Grace Brooks, Alice Eggleston, Alice Smith, Mamie Gray, Flo Gray.

claimed, would parallel that of Spokane, Washington.

"Like Spokane, Smithers will be a great distributing centre and it will have a similarly rapid growth. But in addition to the resources which made Spokane, Smithers has great tributary coal fields and large iron deposits which promise to make it a steel-manufacturing city."

On the contrary, the war all but ended immigration to the area, and with conscription in effect, actually occasioned the departure of many of the valley's young men. This, in turn, caused serious shortages of farm help which became a critical problem at harvest time. Reports of crop losses due to labor shortages were numerous during the war. At one point in July 1918, valley farmers actually passed a resolution calling upon the authorities to "close down all non-essential work, including quartz and coal prospecting and road work for the harvest months," thereby enabling workers in these areas to labor in the fields.

Even established farmers were not exempt from the call to war, many of them having to face government tribunals to explain why they should not be forced to enlist. Among those called before one tribunal, located in Telkwa, was young Axel Elmsted who, in June of 1918, was given one month to put his farm in order before leaving. Late in the war, attempts were made to recruit farm labor from among the merchants, carpenters and rail workers in the town. L.B. Warner, who took over publication of the Interior News in 1918, thus editorialized: ". . . the labor situation has become so acute that it is absolutely essential that while these men [soldiers] are holding the first line trench of civilization, we in Smithers and other towns take up their work in the fields . . . " He then volunteered his entire staff, himself, for the job at hand.

Despite such pleas, it's unlikely the townsfolk of Smithers put much of a dent in the farmers' collective workload. According to a census taken by the community's registrar (and later its jeweller and bandmaster) J.S. Gray, the population of Smithers in the summer of 1918 stood at 312 persons over the age of 16 years. Hardly the new Spokane of the North!

The Roman Catholic Church at the corner of Queen and First.

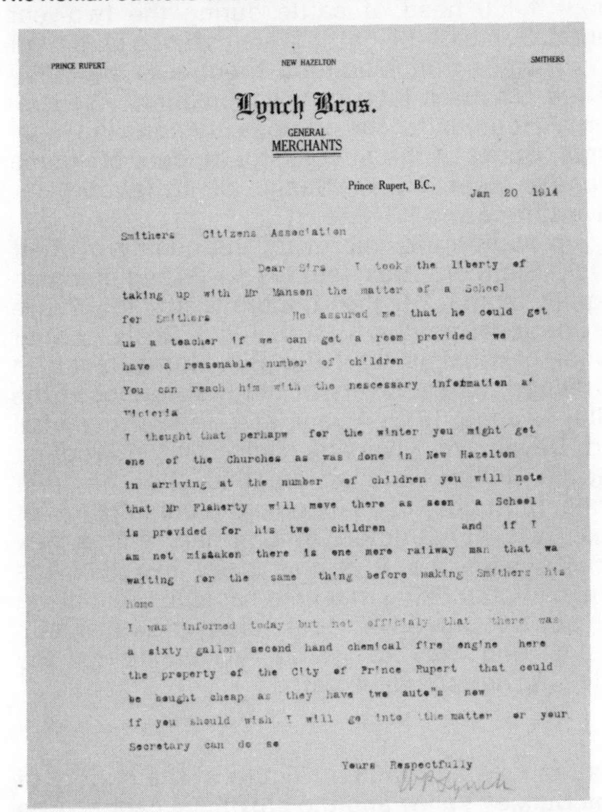

PRINCE RUPERT NEW HAZELTON SMITHERS

Lynch Bros.

GENERAL
MERCHANTS

Prince Rupert, B.C., Jan 20 1914

Smithers Citizens Association

Dear Sirs I took the liberty of taking up with Mr Manson the matter of a School for Smithers He assured me that he could get us a teacher if we can get a room provided we have a reasonable number of children
You can reach him with the nescessary infotmation at Victoria
I thought that perhapw for the winter you might get one of the Churches as was done in New Hazelton
in arriving at the number of children you will note that Mr Flaherty will move there as soon a School is provided for his two children and if I am not misaaken there is one more railway man that wa waiting for the same thing before making Smithers his home
I was informed today but not officialy that there was a sixty gallon second hand chemical fire engine here the property of the City of Prince Rupert that could be bought cheap as they have two auto"s now
if you should wish I will go into the matter or your Secretary can do so

Yours Respectfully

H P Lynch

The need for a school and fire protection was an early priority as witnessed by this letter from H.P. Lynch, President of the Citizens Association.

Some of the fine agricultural land in the Bulkley Valley. This farm later became part of the Experimental Farm.

However, settlement on a limited scale did occur. In finally realizing the potential of the valley, the provincial government designated 24,000 acres on the east side of the Bulkley River as its first settlement area in the province. The designation, made under terms of B.C.'s new Land Settlement Act, included existing farms, soldiers' holdings and previous Boer War scrip, accounting for about 8,000 acres. The remaining 16,000 acres were to be divided into 160-acre farms, thereby accommodating up to 100 new families.

The optimism engendered by that settlement plan was never rewarded. Five years later only 924 acres had been sold, representing seven new families. Locally, much of the blame was laid at the feet of the government which, for many years, failed to provide a land locator. Prospective settlers would arrive in the valley only to find that no one had ever really surveyed the farm lots. As one settler put it: "Why is the provincial government hiding its light under a bushel? A land locator is the logical remedy for the existing evil, and no time should be lost in making the necessary appointment . . ." According to that same settler, who shared his anger with Interior News readers, "scores of intending settlers were driven out because of no means of ascertaining where the land was to be found, either for purchase or by homestead."

The second major settlement scheme of this time was that of the Rattenbury Land Company. As mentioned previously, Sir Francis Mawson Rattenbury had purchased several thousand acres in the valley at about the same time the G.T.P. announced its intentions to construct the railroad. Much of the money used to purchase the land had been earned by Rattenbury in his capacity as architect on the provincial parliament buildings and the Empress Hotel in Victoria. His land investment was a purely speculative venture which would require completion of the rail line in order to succeed. However, just as Rattenbury was about to cash in on his land, Canada went to war. As Terry Reksten reported in her book, *Rattenbury,* "the land became a burden . . . tens of thousands of undeveloped acres on which he would have to pay taxes and from which he could expect no return." He did sell some of his property, mostly through the efforts of Mr. John Wood, his agent in Telkwa, who divided his time between the valley and promotional tours of the Canadian Prairies, Great Britian and the United States. Actual figures on the numbers of settlers drawn to the valley by Rattenbury promotional efforts are not available. But it is known that thousands of acres of Rattenbury's land went unsold, despite the company's later amalgamation, for promotional purposes, with the United Grain Growers and a number of B.C. land companies. In fact, almost all of his unsold acreage reverted to the Crown in 1927, two years before he and his second wife, who was much younger than he, left B.C. forever to settle in England.*

Francis Mawson Rattenbury, cira 1924. B.C. Provincial Archives photo.

Rattenbury, however, and a number of other land agents operating in the valley did not go completely without success. Between 1918 and 1920 the valley's population rose from 1,000 to 1,500. Newspaper reports from this time record the arrival of 94 carloads of settlers' effects and about 1,400 head of cattle during the two-year period. Some of the cattle were part of a shipment of purebreds from Manitoba, brought to the valley by the Northern Interior Stockbreeders Association of Houston for the purpose of improving local herds. Some of the successful bidders for these animals were J.C.K. Sealy, of Driftwood, H. Silverthorne and T.T. Aitken.

In addition to improving the quality of their stock, Smithers area farmers were beginning to acquire some of the trappings of the more conventional southern farms. Jack Sealy, former owner of what is now the Bill Morris ranch in Driftwood, took delivery of the first tractor in the valley in June, 1918. A year later Sealy, Rosenthal and Devoin of Riverside Dairy and newcomer George Oulton were all erecting silos on their farms. In August of 1920, a cold storage plant for meat was constructed in Smithers and a few months later the Riverside dairy installed the valley's first milking machine capable of "milking two cows at one time." Technology, however, still had a long way to go as evidenced by the following newspaper excerpt.

*Rattenbury, a prominent figure in the history of the Bulkley Valley and the provincial capital, was later murdered by his chauffeur who had become Mrs. Rattenbury's lover. She committed suicide shortly thereafter.

The Carr Ranch, located just east of Sealy's corner on the Babine Lake Road.

"Charlie Chapman was in Smithers on Wednesday (Nov. 27, 1918) and reports threshing operations drawing to a close throughout the valley and especially in the Glentanna section . . . A unique spectacle was to be seen in connection with threshing during the past two weeks. Much of the grain was still shocked in the fields and the snow of recent precipitation made it possible, even advisable, to haul the sheaves to the threshing machine on sleighs."

Despite the fact they were "caught out in the cold" that year, valley farmers were coming up with very creditable grain production. Charlie Chapman produced a total of 260,000 pounds that fall, followed by William Croteau of Telkwa with 177,675 pounds and F.M. Dockrill, also of Telkwa, with 137,069 pounds. The yields of most area farmers for that fall were later published in the Interior News. Many of their names are familiar even today.

William Croteau
F.M. Dockrill
Jos. Bourgon
E. Barger
Fay Short
F.G. Heal
G. McDonell
Robt. M. Burns
J.C.K. Sealy
A.J. Prudhomme
G. Lacroix
Tom Herlihy
R. Wakefield
E. Heal
J. Goodwill
R.E. Williams
E. Morin
J. Gray
P. Regan
G. Oulton
E. Wakefield
E. Heal
R. Barger
Bert Heal
J.J. Bakke
P. White
P. Moran
J. Aitken
J. Oullet
J. Basin
C.E. Thoman
I. Short
Joe French
Wm. Cocks
Wm. Johnson
Geo. Moore
H. Fink
J.T. More
W. Wakefield
E. Lemieux
H. Miller
T. Brewer
John Lapadat
John Meaney
Charles Newitt

In May of 1919, F.A. Gilbert of Stettler, Alberta, purchased the 320-acre Pat McFee farm in Driftwood and just over a year later the Kidd family arrived from Red Deer Alberta, purchasing the Gregory farm just across the Bulkley River, a short distance from Smithers. The valley's farming community, needless to say, was a strong one having a collective voice in the Bulkley Valley Farmers' Institute. One of the earliest requests made by the institute was for an experimental farm to be located in this area. The first mention of this came in 1918 and was later the subject of several editorials by Interior News editor L.B. Warner who argued for the farm as an asset to returning soldiers eager to make their living from the land. Despite several promises from federal MP's, it was to be several years before the experimental farm, now the Northern Training Centre, was established by Ottawa. It should be noted that even without the obvious advantages of an experimental farm, valley produce was already in demand in other parts of the province. A large order for B.V. timothy seed was placed in 1920 by

Haying at the Carr Ranch. Farming and ranching were major contributors to the local economy in the early years and have continued to be an important industry in the valley ever since.

Vancouver Island farmers attempting to improve their hay quality and in the following year the same commodity was awarded first prize at the Victoria seed fair.

As stated earlier, members of tne prospecting fraternity were among the first visitors to the valley to admire both its physical attractiveness and potential as a source of income. As early as 1892 the surveyor, A.L. Poudrier, in recommending a road be built to the area to facilitate settlement, made mention of coal outcroppings west of Telkwa as well as the possibility of gold and silver properties. According to one source, one of the first claims staked in the valley was in 1899 on Goat Creek, a tributary of the Telkwa River and eventual site of a mine which, at best, produced enough coal for local consumption. Frank Dockrill, later a prominent farmer in the Telkwa area, staked some of the early Telkwa River claims in 1905, leaving a written record of his prospecting trip. The following is an excerpt from his own manuscript, published in the book *Skeena - River of Destiny* by Dr. Large.

"Prospectors and land seekers were arriving daily and we learned that a general store was to be opened on the bench by two men named Lem Broughton and Jack McNeil, which assured us of a place to renew our supplies when we would return from the hills.

"With the aid of our Indian canoes, we swam our horses across the Bulkley River and started West for the mountains known as Hunter Basin, named after an old prospector who had staked claims there the year before.* After spending some time looking over the mountains in the Hunter Basin area, we continued west crossing Glacier Creek on to Sunset Creek. Here we spent some time and staked some claims showing copper ore then continued on west across Gold Creek and Dominion Basin. Evidences of copper ore were found on almost every range but nothing outstanding . . . On our way up the north fork of the Maurice [Morice] we found coal float and followed it for miles, finally entering Gold Stream, and followed the float into what we later called Coal Creek and near the head of this small creek we found a nice seam of high grade bituminous coal which later proved to be seven feet thick. After staking six sections of coal lands, we procured generous samples, for by this time our packhorse was travelling light, and headed for the Bulkley Valley . . . After laying in the valley for a while we headed for Hazelton, as at that time the steamer did not run late into fall, owing to low water and lack of business. At Hazelton we made arrangements for the wintering of our packhorse

*William Hunter arrived in the Bulkley Valley about 1903, staked the Hunter Basin claim in 1904, and lived in the district until the fall of 1917 when he left for the United States. He died a year later in Nevada in a mining accident.

and, in the meantime, having a generous supply of coal samples, we optioned our coal claims to some Butte (Montana) interests. We later took the last trip of the river steamer to Port Essington and the coast steamer for Vancouver."

A year later, in 1906, four companies — Cassiar Coal Company, Kitimat Development Syndicate, Trans-Continental Development Syndicate and Telkwa Milling and Development Company — were all examining coal properties in the Goat Creek area. There was some development work done after that but even by 1918, twelve years later, there had still been no real production. It was in that year Prince Rupert interests obtained the Goat Creek properties, with promises that shipping would begin by early summer. By September there still hadn't been any shipment, due to poor road conditions to the mine and inadequate rail facilities. During the course of the next year only 1.75 tons were extracted and in 1921 the Telkwa Colleries shut down for two years. Production was sporadic for the next several years. In fact, actual mineral production, of any kind, never really amounted to much in the valley with the exception of the Silver Standard Mine in Hazelton, the Duthie Mine on Hudson Bay Mountain and the Cronin lease in the Babine Mountains.

The original ore discovery on Hudson Bay Mountain is said to have been made by an Indian girl about 1900. She was apparently hunting goats with her father when she noticed some glittering bits of rock. They brought the fragments down off the mountain and later sold them to the Hankin brothers who had several good claims in the Goat Creek area. This find was followed three years later when John Halley, Jabez Ashman and William Boyd staked several claims on the mountain and removed about five tons of ore for assay. The ore, packed out by the Charleson and Barrett pack train, proved valuable and precipitated a staking rush in the area. These claims later became well known as the Victory Mine, the Mamie group, Silver Peak Group, the Carolina and Last Chance claims, the Empire Group and several others.

Perhaps the best known of these was the Mamie Group, eight claims on the southwest slope of the mountain, that were obtained by J.F. Duthie, a Seattle shipbuilder, in 1919. Development work on these claims began just weeks after Duthie got them but it was to be four years before workers hit a rich vein and began shipping ore regularly.

Meanwhile, on the other side of the Bulkley River in the Babine Mountains, mining developer James Cronin had obtained a lease on what would eventually become another of the valley's three operating mines. Cronin, who had previously put two other B.C. mines into operation, spent from 1907 to 1923 developing the Babine Bonanza for production, investing about $200,000 of his own money. In 1916 the province put up $30,000 for the

Cronin Mine in the Babine mountains in the early 1900's.

Many hardships and mishaps were associated with mining as the story of Jack Pekoe illustrates. Pekoe carried the mail into the Cronin Mine. He would go into Silverking basin, cross over into Hyland basin and then down to the mine. In the winter of 1915-16, he was reported missing. He was caught in a sudden snowslide and died. Several attempts to look for him were made, but snow conditions and the large snowslide on the trail made a thorough search impossible until spring. His body was found the following July and carried out by Chief Constable John Kelly of the B.C. Provincial police (left) and local packer Jack Henry (right).

road into the mine site. Cronin himself was injured on the site in 1923, just as the mine went into production. He never fully recovered from his injuries and died in 1925. The mine was closed down and was not re-opened until three years later under new ownership.

Despite the actual lack of any real mineral production in the valley during the first two decades of the century, there was no shortage of claim staking, road building, colorful characters, and optimistic forecasts of future wealth. A conservative count of properties being developed during the early twenties would stand at about 20. In addition to those already mentioned, there were at least eight major groups in the Babines, one belonging to C.G. (Peavine) Harvey who worked his Harvey Mountain claim well into his eighties. Peavine was also responsible, in 1918, for formation of the Smithers Miners Association. Other S.M.A. members included Donald Simpson (Simpson's Gulch), long associated with the Empire and Victory properties on Hudson Bay Mountain and J.S. (Kicker) Kelly who spent a good portion of his life prospecting in the Bulkley Valley, lending his name to Kelly's Cave on Hudson Bay Mountain and Kelly's Camp on the McCabe trail in the Babines.

In addition to their prospecting, some of these mining men took a keen interest in politics, so much so that in 1920 Kicker Kelly decided to run as an independent against the Hon. A.M. Manson who went on to become the province's Attorney-General. Here's what Kicker had to say about Manson in some abbreviated but unedited campaign literature distributed in early November 1920.

> "he believes in the Patrinege System before election not after."
>
> "him and the Dirty Six advocates that their is knot Brains Enough in the dystrict to represent the People of the dystrict."
>
> "he believes in keeping all Crooks in office for life."

Kicker Kelly's political campaign, 1920. The sign says "Eight Years of Oliver (John Oliver, Premier of B.C.) is enough." To make sure voters got the point, Kelly drew an arrow pointing to the bull below.

> "he Believes in graft and has made more money while surving as member than he has made in the balance of his life."

The eventual outcome of that election was 485 votes for Manson and 32 for Kicker who, as we shall discuss later, spent a few months as a guest of the government at Oakalla Prison.

Also interested in politics was A.P. (Red) McCabe who may have acquired his nickname in connection with his role as secretary of the local chapter of the Socialist Party of Canada. McCabe penned the following appeal for funds in 1919.

"Local Smithers 97, S.P.O.C. sends out an appeal for funds for the purpose of building a hall in Smithers. The long winter nights will soon be here; hence our desire to build a place in which the workers will be able to acquire the knowledge essential to a true understanding of their class position in a modern capitalist society . . . ."

Most of Red McCabe's prospecting activity was conducted in the Babines where, in 1920, he completed the five bridges across Driftwood Creek. He is also responsible for what is now the well-known hiking trail along the back side of Harvey Mountain. Another of the prominent, early prospectors was P.J. (Paddy) Higgins who originally staked the Silver King claim in 1916 and was later involved in development of the Victory claim on Hudson Bay Mountain.

In addition to mining and agriculture, the making of railway ties was another key component in the valley's economic base. From Terrace to Houston this particular industry was dominated by Olof Hanson, B.C.'s Swedish Counsel for 32 years and the federal Member of Parliament for this area for 15 years. Hanson opened his first office in Prince Rupert in 1906, managing both his tie cutting business and a cedar pole export operation. At its peak, about

Ernie Heal (standing) and friend unloading railroad ties from a sled. Many early residents made their living from the tie cutting industry.

1919, the Hanson Tie Co., with a seasonal office in Smithers was filling orders from the G.T.P. for up to 500,000 ties annually. Two groups of men were involved in this operation; the professional tie hackers who operated out of railside camps and the "stump farmers." According to one newspaper account from 1919, Hanson had 300 men, many of them transient workers, employed at 20 camps in the valley. Area settlers soon discovered they could augment meagre incomes by producing ties from trees on their own land. More than one area stump farmer managed to survive the depression in this way, working either for Hanson interests or one of the other contractors. During good years it was not unusual for more than a million ties to be produced in the valley. Hanson, who opened his permanent Smithers office in 1925 in what is now the Apollo Automotive building, died in Vancouver in 1952.

Actual lumber production in the valley was another source of employment in the early days though to a considerably lesser extent than tie making. One of the first mills was established at Telkwa in 1907 by William Croteau, Jos. Bourgon and Tom Thorpe. The first large scale mill in the Telkwa area, belonging to Geoffrey McDonell, opened early in 1920, near the present site of Eddy Park, and had a capacity of 10,000 feet per day. In Smithers, the Williams-Carr Lumber Co. was established in 1913 and was taken over the following year by George Little, regarded as the founder of Terrace. This business eventually became Smithers Lumber Yard, located at the corner of Queen and Alfred. Smithers was also the site of the Northern B.C. Lumber Company. Backed with money from Calgary business interests, the mill opened in 1920 with a capacity of 20,000 board feet a day but lasted only a few weeks before going into receivership. In later years the mill was purchased by other financial interests and became a viable and necessary local industry.

It can be seen then that agriculture, mining, or rather prospecting, tie making and the lumber industry were well established factors in the area's economic stability by the end of World War One. All, of course, were dependent to varying degrees on the G.T.P. rail line which was, in itself, a major industry, providing employment, transportation and, eventually, electric power for the new town. The growth of these industries, however, was not something accomplished without great hardship and, very often tragedy. In retrospect, we often tend to emphasize, and occasionally romanticize, the accomplishments of our pioneers without ever realizing the costs.

In connection with the early days of the railway, for instance, serious accidents were a weekly occurrence. In one three week period, between April 6, 1918 and the end of the month,

Telkwa, B.C. with the G.M. McDonell sawmill in the foreground, circa 1913.

Bob Burns, Clary Goodacre and Hughie Heal (L-R), employees of McDonell's sawmill in Telkwa (present Eddie Park site).

Fires were a constant threat in the early days. This one was in Telkwa in 1913.

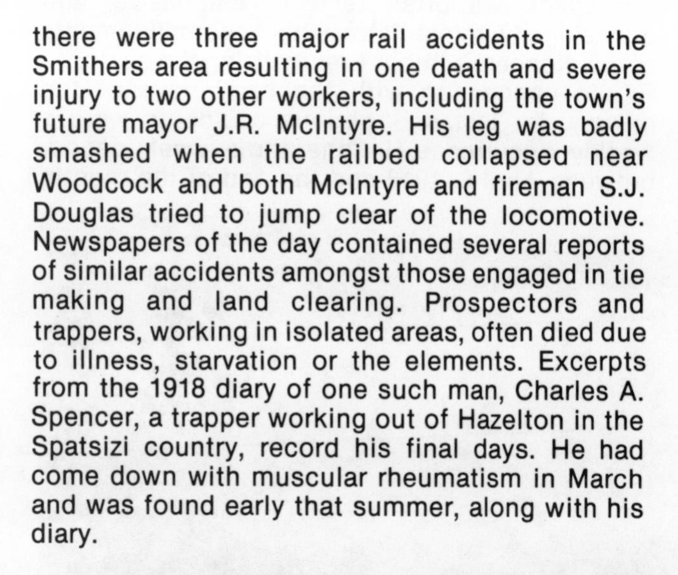

there were three major rail accidents in the Smithers area resulting in one death and severe injury to two other workers, including the town's future mayor J.R. McIntyre. His leg was badly smashed when the railbed collapsed near Woodcock and both McIntyre and fireman S.J. Douglas tried to jump clear of the locomotive. Newspapers of the day contained several reports of similar accidents amongst those engaged in tie making and land clearing. Prospectors and trappers, working in isolated areas, often died due to illness, starvation or the elements. Excerpts from the 1918 diary of one such man, Charles A. Spencer, a trapper working out of Hazelton in the Spatsizi country, record his final days. He had come down with muscular rheumatism in March and was found early that summer, along with his diary.

> "I have now been here close on one month, and have not been able to leave the cabin. When I am lying down and warm, I seem to feel no pain but Oh God, when I get up and try to cook something for myself the pain is unbearable. I have been able to cook but one hotcake a day for myself. If I only had someone to cook for me I might be alright. At times it seems the struggle to live is too hard. Now; whoever finds this try to find my furs."

Wooden building materials and the absence of any effective fire fighting equipment resulted in much property destruction, as opposed to just damage, and loss of life. Physical injury often led to suicide, mostly among men incapacitated and unable to work for long periods of time. Loneliness, monotonous work and isolation, all familiar to valley pioneers, also led to numerous suicides which, unlike today, were reported in detail by newspaper editors. A number of the valley's earliest residents ended their lives in this way.

Injuries and illness in the valley, at least during the first two decades of settlement, were an extremely serious matter as doctors were few, transportation slow and often hazardous, and health facilities ill-equipped. When influenza hit the valley late in 1918, Dr. H.C. Wrinch of Hazelton was the only doctor between Terrace and Vanderhoof. That epidemic, despite Dr. Wrinch's heroic efforts to minimize its effects, claimed the lives of about a dozen valley residents, including that of Roman Malkow, brother of Glentanna rancher Dymtro Malkow.

Along with its joys, birth always carries some measure of pain. And those who built the town of Smithers and settled its adjacent lands had their share of pain. They also shared no end of resourcefulness and the occasional bit of humor, as evidenced by the following newspaper report of conditions in the Smithers public school which had been converted to a hospital during the influenza epidemic.

> "Nurse 'Peavine' Harvey is doing noble service and having the time of his young life on the day shift but the night nurse, Jas. Kennedy [owner of a local pool hall] complains that his co-worker talks the patients into a comatose state by noon and that they only come out of it at night in time to keep him on the jump. This, Mr. Kennedy thinks, should be against the rules of the house."

Charlie Morris, who then operated a butcher shop on the present day flea-market site, served as the cook at the improvised hospital.

The Red Cross picnic, Lake Kathlyn, Sunday, August 8, 1915.

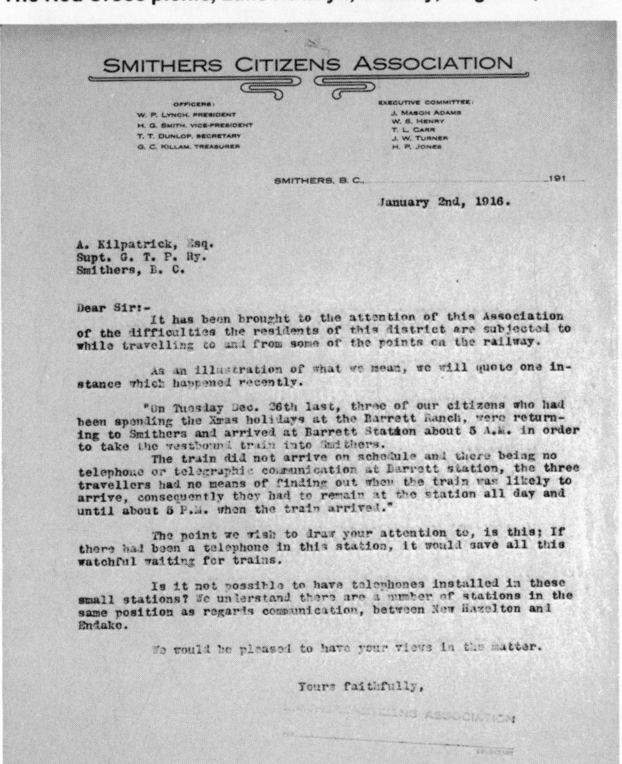

SMITHERS CITIZENS ASSOCIATION

OFFICERS:
W. P. LYNCH, PRESIDENT
H. G. SMITH, VICE-PRESIDENT
T. T. DUNLOP, SECRETARY
G. C. KILLAM, TREASURER

EXECUTIVE COMMITTEE:
J. MASON ADAMS
W. S. HENRY
T. L. CARR
J. W. TURNER
H. P. JONES

SMITHERS, B. C. ____191

January 2nd, 1916.

A. Kilpatrick, Esq.
Supt. G. T. P. Ry.
Smithers, B. C.

Dear Sir:-

It has been brought to the attention of this Association of the difficulties the residents of this district are subjected to while travelling to and from some of the points on the railway.

As an illustration of what we mean, we will quote one instance which happened recently.

"On Tuesday Dec. 26th last, three of our citizens who had been spending the Xmas holidays at the Barrett Ranch, were returning to Smithers and arrived at Barrett Station about 5 A.M. in order to take the westbound train into Smithers.

The train did not arrive on schedule and there being no telephone or telegraphic communication at Barrett station, the three travellers had no means of finding out when the train was likely to arrive, consequently they had to remain at the station all day and until about 5 P.M. when the train arrived."

The point we wish to draw your attention to, is this; If there had been a telephone in this station, it would save all this watchful waiting for trains.

Is it not possible to have telephones installed in these small stations? We understand there are a number of stations in the same position as regards communication, between New Hazelton and Endako.

We would be pleased to have your views in the matter.

Yours faithfully,

SMITHERS CITIZENS ASSOCIATION

Travelling in the Bulkley Valley had its difficulties. One such problem was the subject of this complaint to G.T.P. Superintendent Kilpatrick from the Citizens Association.

Railroading, 1921. L-R: B.J. Walkland, Roy Lawcett, Tom Cullen and George Raymond.

KRAUS
Portion of Smithers B.C.

CHAPTER 3

B.C.'s First Village

With nurses the likes of James Kennedy and Peavine Harvey, who was well over 50 at the time of the influenza epidemic, it's safe to say the provision of health care in Smithers still had a long way to go. In other areas, however, the new town was definitely maturing. During the course of the war, which ended in November, 1918, Smithers had traded its Squatterville image for one of permanence and was now poised for a decade of growth and prosperity.

Advertisements contained in issues of the Interior News from November, 1918, provide a sketch of the town's business community. R.S. Sargent was now operating general stores in Hazelton, Telkwa and Smithers and advertising 10 per cent discounts on all goods purchased by returning soldiers. Another general store, operated by S.A. (Sam) Eby and located where the Royal Bank now stands, promised a new shipment of chinaware in time for Christmas. Mr. Eby's brother, Ed, later opened a hardware store which eventually became Rodgers' Hardware. Patrons of J. Mason Adams' drug store, located in what is now the Central Clothing building, were being urged to purchase the new electric flashlight "as a matter of self-protection as well as convenience." Sealy and Doodsons' butcher shop on Main Street, now the site of Smithers Hardware, was offering a fine selection of beef, mutton, pork, veal, eggs, fresh and smoked fish, and chickens. No less than four real estate agents were offering their services to potential property owners. In addition to his pool room, James Kennedy was offering "fresh fruit in season" and a circulating library. The Empress Barber Shop saw to the town's tonsorial requirements while George K. Katsuro provided baths for ladies and gentlemen as well as a laundry service. Tom Fushimi later acquired the laundry which still carries his name, Tom's Laundry, and remains in its original Broadway Avenue location. J.S. Gray, watch inspector for the G.T.P., was now operating his jewellery store. The George Little Lumber Yards at Queen and Alfred offered double dressed, clear cedar for $60 a thousand feet while either Bulkley Transfer Stables (Beaton and Hoops) or Auto Stage Cartage (T. Herlihy) would haul the lumber home for you. L.L. Devoin and Gustav Rosenthal looked to the town's dairy needs from their Riverside Dairy on the Bulkley River. Other services and commodities available in the

Sargent's Store at the corner of First and Main. City Transfer, in the foreground, making its merchandise deliveries.

J.Mason Adams Drug Store at the corner of Main and Second. The small addition on the right housed the post office until the mid 1950's. Adams started his business in the tent behind his store. The original building is still in use, being presently occupied by Central Clothing.

The interior of J. Mason Adams Drug Store.

Kennedy's Pool Room. Located on Main Street between Alfred and Broadway (present Wall Electric site), it was a popular place.

Smithers of late 1918 included blacksmithing, farm implements, insurance policies of all kinds and a music store where Mrs. L.B. (Peg) Warner, wife of the local newspaper publisher, sold Edison and Victor phonographs and records, violins, banjos, guitars and sheet music. In addition to his editorial pursuits, L.B. Warner also served as the local stationer, supplying typewriters, rubber stamps and a "complete line" of bookkeeping materials. Ernie Hann was advertising his skills as a carpenter, the hardware store wanted customers for its doll buggies and rocking horses and D.A. McRae, proprietor of the Good Eats Grill was serving a "merchants lunch" for 50 cents a plate.

The hotel business in Smithers, somewhat dormant during the war years, now entered a period of much activity and, in two instances, disaster. Three major hotels - The Bulkley, The City and The Royal - were operating by 1919. The City Hotel, owned by James Kotow, and The Royal, owned by H.D. Gazanoff and operated by D.A. McRae, were located side by side on Alfred Avenue. At about 9:00 P.M. on September 26, 1921, both buildings were levelled by fire despite the fact that almost every citizen of the town and even a trainload of G.T.P. passengers joined in the fight to save the two wooden structures. There were no injuries even though 40 guests were registered at the time.

Within months two new buildings were up near the same site. A rooming house, named the Hotel Evelyn, opened on October 24 with 14 rooms and on February 20, 1922, H.D. Gazanoff opened his new Hotel Dage right next door. This building, later known as the Smithers Hotel, was lost in a fire April 26, 1932.

The Bulkley Hotel officially opened for business July 8, 1918. Owned by R.E. Williams, of the original Williams-Carr Lumber Co., the Bulkley was sold about one year later. The new owner was E.E. (Ed) Orchard who operated the hotel for several years in addition to his many civic

An inside view of the Empress Billiards Parlor at the corner of Alfred and Main.

The Red Front Store and the real estate office next door, two early Main Street businesses.

The Bulkley Hotel. The model "T"s are lined up for a race down Main Street — an early version of the drag race.

responsibilities, including six years as Smithers' mayor. Although it has undergone major renovations, internally and externally, the original Bulkley Hotel is still a prominent Main Street structure.

At about the same time as the Smithers hotel industry was hitting its stride, a limited form of prohibition came into effect, whereby the only legal liquor dispenser was the government agent, Stephen H. Hoskins. As such, it was not uncommon to hear that certain public house proprietors had been arrested for supplying an additional service to their patrons. Such was the fate of Messrs. Gazanoff, McRae and James Kennedy in the summer of 1922. The bootlegging of homemade spirits was also a "problem" during this period and one to which Interior News publisher L.B. Warner devoted considerable space. The issue of July 7, 1920 contained one of his more eloquent criticisms of this practise.

> "Citizens of Smithers who were enjoying the calm and cool of Sunday evening were forced to witness exhibitions of drunkenness and profanity that would have done credit to the best efforts of the bar room's balmiest days. Ladies on the way home from church were, in several cases, forced to walk on the road to evade the reeling, bleery-eyed rats who were again victims of the greed that has taken possession of would-be reputable citizens who vie with each other in their efforts and boasts of establishing the rule of Soapy Smith. When men can peddle rotten liquor and boast of the slowness of Canadian officials it is about time that Canadians stepped in and demon-

Mr. and Mrs. Stephen H. Hoskins on their 50th wedding anniversary in 1959. Hoskins was government agent in Hazelton before moving to Smithers.

strated that there is a difference between forbearance and fear, and that they must not confuse our tolerance of their methods to a degree with slowness. Decent people have a right to the free use of our sidewalks without being subject to the indignity of the leers of a gang of slobbering bohunks jinned up by a lot of yellow skunks slinking behind skirts and other frailties and calling themselves 'slick.' "

It is likely Mr. Warner was a staunch supporter of The Moderation League of B.C. which, at the time, was advocating "the inculcation of true temperance principles consistent with personal liberty." In any case, tippling was but one diversion available to residents of post-war Smithers. In addition to Mrs. Warner's Music Store, culture buffs could avail themselves of productions by the Smithers Choral and Dramatic Society formed in 1919 with an executive which included Mrs. Warner, Mrs. S.A. Eby, Miss Jean Grant (Mrs. Jean Kilpatrick), Miss Ethel Kilpatrick and Mr. Harry Eden. The Society's first production, apparently an early tribute to biculturalism, was entitled "Ici On Parle Francais." The Smithers Moving Picture House, managed by Wiggs O'Neill, opened for business April 2, 1920, showing Charlie Chaplin's "The Tramp." Chautaquas, travelling variety shows, were another popular form of entertainment. The 12-act show which visited Telkwa, Smithers and Prince Rupert in the summer of 1921 included a violinist, a group calling themselves The Old-Fashioned Girls and two speakers who addressed themselves to the "History of English Speaking Races Since Columbus" and "What Democracy Means To Me." Dances, too, were another regular pastime although getting to the out-of-town ones often presented a problem. One such outing, to a dance in Telkwa, produced the following newspaper report.

Norman and Jean Kilpatrick, Easter Sunday, 1923. Mr. Kilpatrick was Smithers' postmaster for many years and son of Allan Kilpatrick, G.T.P. Superintendent. Mrs. Kilpatrick, the former Miss Jean Grant, was active in the Smithers Choral and Dramatic Society.

"All was not merry and bright with the several sleighing parties that left Smithers for the Red Cross dance in Telkwa on Monday night. The jubilation of one load expired at the big hill two miles out of town. The hill was bare of snow and obstructed by a mudslide and in attempting to surmount this difficulty, a trace parted, but not so with hope. A liberal supply of neckties, shoe laces and miscellaneous articles were pressed into service and all seemed well. The first attempt to move, however, proved otherwise, for it was found that the whiffletrees had broken, and the faces radiant with expectancy were thrown into despair. The trip was cancelled and the party lameducked to town with nothing but a liberal supply of gumbo as momento of a big event."

Smithers, as can be seen from preceding newspaper excerpts, was also extremely fortunate in having a newspaper editor of L.B. Warner's calibre. He was obviously a man of wit, humour and strongly held opinions, all of which were, for more than 20 years, eloquently expressed on the pages of The Interior News. L.B., as he was known to his friends, arrived in Smithers early in 1918, taking over the paper from Joseph L. Coyle. (Coyle, who had spent a dozen years in the valley as a journalist, moved to Vancouver where he invented and patented the egg crate. By early 1919 his factory was producing 5,000 of the crates a day and still falling far short of local demand, let alone the interest being expressed throughout the rest

Larry B. Warner, Editor of the Interior News. A very active man, he served the community in many ways, including a stint as Chairman of the Village Commissioners, 1930-31.

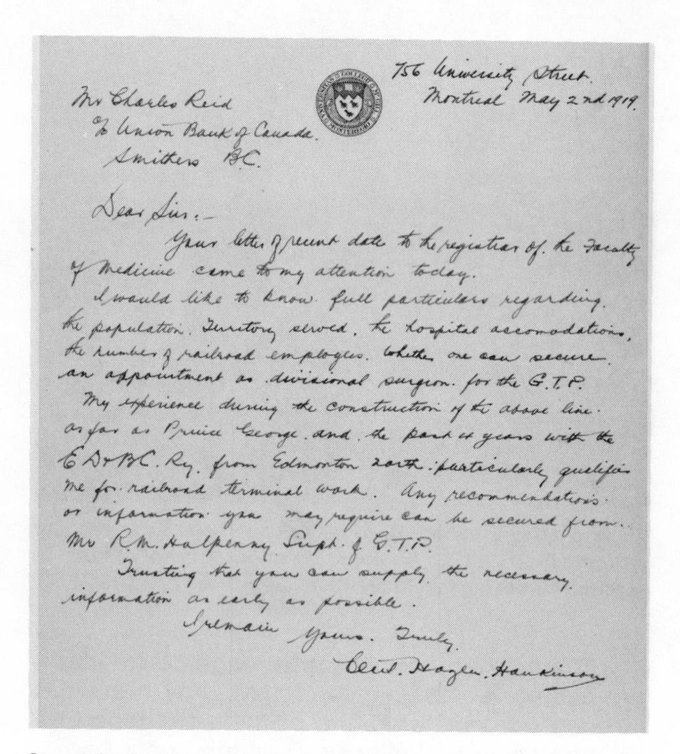

756 University Street.
Montreal May 2nd 1919.

Mr Charles Reid
c/o Union Bank of Canada.
Smithers B.C.

Dear Sir:-

Your letter of recent date to the registrar of the Faculty of Medicine came to my attention today.

I would like to know full particulars regarding the population. Territory served, the hospital accomodations, the number of railroad employees. Whether one can secure an appointment as divisional surgeon for the G.T.P.

My experience during the construction of the above line as far as Prince George. and the past [illegible] years with the E.D.&B.C. Ry. from Edmonton north. particularly qualifies me for railroad terminal work. Any recommendations or information you may require can be secured from Mr R.M. Halpenny Supt. of G.T.P.

Trusting that you can supply the necessary information as early as possible.

I remain Yours Truly.
[illegible] Hagen. Hankinson

Surprisingly, there was a great deal of response to an ad requesting the services of a doctor for the remote and largely undeveloped Bulkley Valley. This letter is from Dr. C.H. Hankinson in far-away Montreal. Hankinson took the job and served the area for many years.

of Canada and in Europe. Coyle remained a close friend of Larry Warner's and, for some years, The Interior News office served as the primary outlet in the valley for Coyle's egg crates). In addition to his role as newspaper publisher and editor, Warner served for a number of years as Secretary to the local School Board and the Bulkley Valley Fall Fair. He was an active member of the Board of Trade and, both editorially and in a more direct way, became one of the strongest proponents of the town's incorporation which became a reality in December of 1921.

Warner was also an avid supporter of improved health facilities for the new town and began campaigning in this direction early in his newspaper career. His forthrightness is evidenced in the following report from a Citizens' Association meeting held in April of 1919. The account also contains what may be one of the first references to the town's infamous drainage ditch which ran the length of Main Street.

> "To accent the general depressing situation presented by the lack of a doctor in this district, Nurse Campbell appeared at Tuesday's meeting of citizens to support her communication directed against the unsanitary condition about town. Nurse Campbell attributed the outbreak of throat infection among the children to poor drainage and accumulated rubbish in the big ditch ..... President A. Kilpatrick then outlined the steps that had been taken by the association to protect the health of the community and it was shown where the health authorities at Victoria were investigating. It was decided to give the latter a kick in the ribs to get action."

It is not known whether this particular treatment remedied the situation in Victoria, but the town did get its first permanent doctor on July 19, 1919 when Dr. C.H. Hankinson, a graduate of McGill University in Montreal, took up residence. Previous health care was provided by Hazelton's Dr. H.C. Wrinch who had visited once a week, setting up office above J. Mason Adams' drug store on Main Street. This location was also used by Dr. Hankinson for a short while prior to his move to the Town Hall. Smithers' first hospital, located on the southwest corner at King Street and Second Avenue, and capable of accommodating about a dozen patients at any one time, was officially opened on September 1, 1920 at a cost of about $6,000. Its first annual report, issued five months later in February, recorded service to 60 patients (57 of whom were "cured") at a total operating deficit of $92.

As stated previously, the community's educational needs had been an early priority, the

The famous (or infamous) Main Street ditch, 1913.

Allan Kilpatrick, Superintendent of the G.T.P., Smithers, 1917-20. Kilpatrick was also active in the Smithers Citizens' Assocation.

Christmas dinner party at the Hospital, 1928. L-R: Fr. Vallier, Dr. Hankinson, nurses McCrostie and Stevenson, Rev. Gibson, Mrs. Hankinson and Bernice Clay.

INSPECTION DEPARTMENT.

PROVINCIAL BOARD OF HEALTH.

VICTORIA, May 6th 1915.

Sir:-

Mr P.deNoe Walker of the Provincial Secretary's Department was recently detailed to visit the northern portion of the Province in order to ascertain the general health conditions. In his report to this department he has made known to us your needs in order to better the sanitary conditions of your embryo city. I may say that the construction of sewers in all unorganized districts is a work that this department never has been called upon to do. The Honourable Doctor Young, however, seems to have sympathetic tendencies in endeavouring to help you out of your apparent sanitary difficulty, and in view of this I take the responsibility of saying that if the citizens and Townsites Company will put up two thirds of the cost, I will recommend that this Department pay the other third providing of course that the total cost does not exceed $1,000.00.

Personally it seems to me that the parties responsible for locating the town in that position should be responsible for its future sanitary welfare.

I have the honour to be,

Sir,

Your obedient servant,

Frank DeGrey

CHIEF INSPECTOR.

H.C.Thompson,Esq.,
Secretary,
Smithers Citizens Ass'n,
Smithers, B.C.

FDG/EG.

Sanitation, particularly the Main Street ditch, was the subject of many a letter between the Citizens Association and the Provincial Government.

June 17th.1915.

T.J.Therp Esq.
Telkwa, B.C.

Dear Sir,-

We beg to advise you, that at a meeting held a short time ago of the Citizens of Smithers, in the interest of a hospital for Bulkley Valley, the following were appointed Board of Directors, Messrs Therp, Christie, of Telkwa; and Lynch, Adams, Gray, Meran and Noel, Smithers, B.C. I have just been informed by Mr Lynch that it is their wish that you should act as secretary for board, and that you write as early as possible to the Provincial Government concerning the matter. If you would kindly call at Adams Drug Store Telkwa And call up Mr Adams Smithers He would be glad to put you in touch with all that transpired at meeting.

Yours very truly

Alex.C.Thomson
Sec. S.Citizens Assc.

Although efforts to bring a hospital to the community were well underway in 1915, it was to be another five years before the first official hospital was actually in operation.

Original Smithers Elementary School. It was located on the present Muheim School site.

A 1915 class in the original Smithers Elementary School. Miss Barwise (extreme right) was the teacher.

first school opening in 1914 in the newly constructed Methodist Church. By December of 1918, school board secretary Warner was advertising for a second teacher to cope with an anticipated post-Christmas enrolment of 50 students, now housed in the new Smithers Public School on Third Avenue. An attendance report for the month of March, 1919, lists the following as students at the school:

Muriel Adams
Harold Berg
Frank Smith
Marjorie Warner
Vera Green
John Williams
Myrtle Berg
Lois Devoin
Robert Dunlop
Harold Fotherby
Oswald Hoskins
Olive Oulton
Freddie Hollinger
Ernest Kirby
Ray Oulton
Daisy Smith
Alice Smith
Gordon Smith
Violet Smith
Gerry Warner
Norman Fotherby
Raymond Moran
Archie St. Louis
Dolphis St. Louis
Nita St. Louis
Johnny Berg
Mamie Gray
Flo Gray
Mary Ellis
Muriel Stephens
Leslie Oulton
Dorothy Devoin
John Devoin
Vera Doodson
Muriel Ellis
Bud Gazeley
Billy Orchard
Nanna Anderson
George Ellis
Harold Ellis
Velma St. Louis

Continued on page 65

An early shot of Smithers, taken from approximately 3rd Avenue, looking west.

Smithers from 2nd Avenue. The Bulkley Hotel was already a prominent feature in the community.

Smithers from 2nd Avenue. This picture was taken from just behind the present Post Office site.

Smithers, looking towards the railway. This picture was taken from the roof of Smithers' first hospital and shows the old St. James Anglican Church in the foreground.

The CNR Station. The station symbolizes the beginnings of Smithers and is still in active service today.

Until the new Provincial Building was constructed in Alfred Park, thereby blocking off Main Street, the CNR Station and the Central Park Building formed "matching book ends" for Main Street.

The Central Park Building. Formerly the Provincial Government Building, it is now a museum and arts centre.

Main Street as it was in the mid-1950s.

Main Street at night - in 1967, Centennial Year.

Main Street and the downtown core as it appears today, after Main Street had its complete facelift in 1979.

The Golden Mile! Smithers and the railroad have historical ties going back to the beginning of this century.

Smithers nestled in the beautiful Bulkley Valley.

The Fall Fair Grounds. The Fall Fair held its 50th consecutive exhibition in 1980. The fair was moved to its present location in 1975.

The Rotary Flea Market - a popular place on summer Saturday mornings.

The Bulkley River - life line of the Bulkley Valley and a source of recreation and enjoyment.

The old Bulkley River bridge. It served Smithers for many years but was demolished in a massive ice jam in 1966.

Hudson Bay Mountain - inseparably linked with Smithers, it is the dominant feature of the area. Think of Smithers and the image of Hudson Bay Mountain instantly comes to mind.

The Silvern Lake area of Hudson Bay Mountain. Scenic areas like this provide residents and visitors alike with abundant recreation opportunities.

Wildlife, such as this deer, is plentiful in the Bulkley Valley.

Hiking on Mount Evelyn, part of the Hudson Bay Mountain area.

Kitseguecla Mountain, better known locally as "The Nipples." Its distinctive shape is recognizable from wherever it can be seen.

Winter in the Bulkley Valley - the crystal clear beauty of untouched snow.

No, its not in the remote northern Hinterlands. This isolated looking scene can be found right in downtown Smithers.

Moricetown Canyon - a well known tourist stop on Highway 16 and an important source of food for the Indian people.

Gaffing the giant spring salmon! Gaffing, as its done at Moricetown, remain basically unchanged from the way it was done generations ago.

The Babine Mountains - another popular recreation area, close to town. Will we have the wisdom and foresight to prevent spoiling these areas so that future generations may enjoy them as well as we?

Majestic Mount Hyland, part of the Babine range.

Hudson Bay Mountain at Lake Kathlyn at the beginning of winter.

Sunset over Lake Kathlyn with Brian Boru peak in the background. This peak is better known locally as "Sleeping Beauty". With a little imagination you can visualize a face in repose in the peak area.

An abandoned and crumbling farm house. What tales this house could tell if only it could speak. Tales of long forgotten dreams, of hardships and labour, of joy and laughter, of sorrow and disappointment . . . tales of the life of the pioneers who built the community we enjoy so much today!

Main Street from Second Avenue.

Main Street between Second and Third Avenue.

By 1921, the school board was accepting applications for a fourth teaching position at the public school and was discussing the possibility of opening a high school. In addition, the Driftwood Public School opened its doors on January 3, 1921.

The need to exchange information also prompted establishment of another learning centre in the valley. Somewhat less formal than the schoolhouse, the Bulkley Valley Agricultural and Industrial Exhibition nevertheless became an institution in the district. The first fall fair, as we

Main Street from Broadway, looking toward the Babine mountains, circa 1914.

Main Street from third Avenue. This picture was taken from in front of the Bulkley Hotel. Automobile traffic was already popular.

The Bulkley Valley Agricultural and Industrial Exhibiton — better known as the Fall Fair — in the 1920's.

The Canadian Legion float passes Henry Motors on Broadway. In the front seat: Bea Monks and "Shorty" Miller. Riding the float (L-R): Bill Henry, Oswald Hoskins, D.A. McRae (of the Smithers Hotel), Charley Monks and Al Finnerty. Henry Motors was located on the present Irly Bird Building Supplies site.

We, whose names are subscribed hereto, being desirous of forming ourselves into an association, to be known as "The Bulkley Valley Agricultural and Industrial Association" under Part II. of the "Agricultural Act," 1915, and Amending Acts, do hereby severally agree to pay to the said Association, yearly, while we continue members of the Association, the membership fee above set forth; and we further agree to conform to the rules and by-laws of the said Association.

DATED this 16th day of June 1919.

Name in Full	Address	Occupation	Annual Subscription.
Signed Alexander C. Prudhomme	Telkwa	Farmer	1.00 pd.
J. G. Wood	Telkwa	Civil Engineer	1.00 pd.
E. C. Barges	"	Farmer	1.00 "
R. E. Williams	Telkwa	Farmer	1.00 pd.
W. S. Henry	Smithers	Broker	1.00 pd.
George Oulton	Smithers	Farmer	1.00 pd.
J.E. Carr	Smithers	Farmer	1.00 pd.
C.O. Chapman	Smithers	Farmer	1.00 pd.
Angus McLean	Smithers	Road Foreman	1.00 pd.
C.S. Daimock	Smithers	Civil Engineer	1.00 pd.
L. B. Warner	"	Publisher	1.00 pd.
Cha. Reid	"	Banker	1.00 pd
J. Mason Adams	"	Druggist	1.00 pd.
A. Kilpatrick	"	Ry. Supt.	1.00 pd.
S.A. Ely	"	Merchant	1.00 pd.
N.P. Moran	Smithers	"	1.00 pd.
Sandy Gozeley	"	Barber	1.00 pd.
Jas. Kotoch	"	Hotelkeeper	1.00 pd.
Ja. Kennedy	"		1.00 pd.
P.J. Hickey	Smithers	Gentlemen	1.00 pd.
E.O. Orchard	"	Hotelkeeper	1.00 Paid
H. Welch	"	Assessor	1.00 Paid
Fred Watons	"	Clerk	1.00 Paid
W. B. Boyer	"	Store Mgr.	1.00 Paid
W. G. Woodsan	"	Butcher	1.00 Paid

The original members of the Bulkley Valley Agricultural and Industrial Association in 1919, each having duly paid his $1.00 membership fee.

know it today, was held September 30, 1919 in the rain near the site of the train station. The directorate for this inaugural event consisted of President A. Kilpatrick, Vice-President J.G. Wood (Rattenbury Lands Co.), Secretary-Treasurer L.B. Warner, George Oulton (farmer), E.C. Barger (farmer), and W.S. Henry (car dealer). A list of 1919 exhibition categories would seem to indicate the fair has changed little, except in size, over the years. The list includes horses, cattle, hogs, goats, poultry, vegetables, grains and grasses, dairy and home produce (cakes, pastry, honey, fruit, canned vegetables, cured meat), ladies' work and minerals. L.B. Warner, in describing the success of the one-day event, stated the people "of town and district can now see the possibilities in connection with an annual fair, and it is the intention to start right in on the preparation for the 1920 event. Grounds are now being secured, a track will be built and the entire show centralized for next year..... This will require unselfish support from the townspeople, it will require preparation from the miners and farmers for exhibiting and it will require plenty of work by those in charge, but from the experience of Tuesday it will be easy to see where all these will be forthcoming."

As it turned out, organizational volunteers were a rare breed in future years, so much so that Editor Warner was constantly having to crusade editorially for support to prevent the early demise of the "annual" event.

While the fall fair provided an opportunity for upgrading agricultural knowledge, it also served to acquaint an increasing number of out-of-town guests with one of the fastest growing communities in the entire district. A visitor to the 1920 edition of the fall fair, for which it also rained, would have witnessed the on-going construction of about six new houses, one of them for G.T.P. engineer and future Smithers mayor, J.R. McIntyre. In travelling to the community he might well have used the newly completed road from Moricetown or arrived via train at the new station completed only months before. That station, which continues in service today, was described in 1919 as a "handsome structure, flooded in light and glory, presenting a picture of beauty that jerked the town from its pioneer air and provided a relieving touch of colour to the inky blackness of Hudson Bay Mountain." In any case it did provide much needed space for G.T.P. employees and passengers and eventually housed the town's first electrical plant.

That same visitor could have bought the latest model car from either W.S. Henry or W.J. (Wiggs) O'Neill, received financial advice from R.L. Gale, legal advice from L.S. McGill, or hired a taxi from G.H. Wall. Had he read the newspaper he might also have gained insight into some of the problems associated with rapid but poorly planned growth, such as that described on the editorial page of the May 12, 1920 Interior News.

> "Right at the present time Smithers is plumb full . . . . Every building is utilized, shacks are the temporary abode of families who would be willing and glad to rent more pretentious buildings, while many men now employed here are compelled to maintain their families in other towns . . . . ."

He might also have encountered this ironic little notice which seems to verify the old adage "the more things change, the more they stay the same."

> "Hereafter all stores in Smithers will be compelled to close air tight on Thursday afternoon and Sundays, the action following an agreement by merchants and a declaration by the government that heavy fines will follow an infraction of the law."

It is not known whether anyone decided to test the law. In any case, the town was definitely experiencing a steady if somewhat problematic period of expansion. As such the Smithers Citizens' Association began meeting with increased frequency, the main subject at most meetings being that of incorporation. The debate over incorporation began late in 1919 and continued, heatedly, for the next two years. At stake was the right of the community to levy its own taxes, thereby raising revenue for a variety of badly needed municipal services, road building among them. However, as the situation stood in 1919, communities such as Smithers were entirely dependent on Victoria for such funds, the division of which most often favoured the more politically powerful southern communities. In one of his first editorials on the matter, L.B. Warner stated the case for Smithers.

> "This community is typical of hundreds of other small places in Omineca and in the province in presenting problems for the solution of which it has no power, and which are purely matters of civic government. We have a light plant that is in private hands and tottering to its fall because there is no authority for collecting street rates as would be provided by an organized village empowered to take over the plant and operate it as a public utility. Water and sewerage systems are necessary, and for want of the privilege of enacting our own laws the burden and expense essential to the upkeep of our streets, sidewalks and totally inadequate fire fighting appliances is borne by a few of the more publicly spirited, while others are free to refuse their share and privileged to grow weeds in their front yards and moss on their backs."

The only remedy for such a condition, according to Warner, was to amend the Municipal Act making provision for the incorporation of villages. Victoria did exactly that one year later but neglected to spell out what new powers incorporation would provide. Consequently, when Smithers petitioned for the right to incorporate in April 1920, being the first community in the province to do so, it took Victoria eight months to draft the initial charter. With receipt of the document began a debate which lasted 1½ years. The original version called for incorporation of an area from the railway to the top of the hill overlooking the river. Three trustees, elected for two year terms, were to constitute the governing body with an administration consisting of a clerk, treasurer and assessor/collector. Trustees would be required to own real property in the village with an assessed value of at least $500.

The powers of the municipality were to include street and sidewalk improvements, drainage, cutting and removal of trees and brush, regulation of traffic on the streets, animals, pounds, nuisances of all kinds, fire protection, fire regulations, lighting and watering of streets, licencing, regulation and inspection of places of amusement and businesses and providing for the poor of the village.

The new municipality would not be allowed to spend more in any year than the incoming revenue for that year. Deficits would be the personal responsibility of the trustees. Borrowing power would be limited to 75 percent of revenue and any money borrowed would have to be repaid during the current year. The municipality would not be allowed to tax government or municipal property, churches, cemeteries, hospitals, poor houses, or property belonging to agricultural societies, and taxes on land and improvements were not to exceed 20 mills.

Also written into the charter was a provision which reflected what amounted to a paranoia amongst white people in the 1920's. No Chinese, Japanese or Indians would be allowed to qualify as voters.

Predictably, debate on the proposed charter centered on finances. Smithers' Methodist Minister, the Rev. James Evans was the most outspoken critic, claiming the sources of revenue and the percentage of that revenue earmarked for the town were insufficient. L.B. Warner, perhaps the strongest advocate of incorporation, argued that while the early years of incorporation might be difficult financially, the move was inevitable, especially since the administrative workload facing the Citizens' Association was increasing daily. He also claimed that even though 80 per cent of the tax money raised by the village would revert to Victoria, the remainder would still amount to more than the village was currently receiving from the Province.

At a public meeting held on February 4, 1921, the citizens of Smithers agreed with Rev. Evans, deciding to postpone any further action on their request for incorporation. It was an obvious disappointment for L.B. Warner who penned the following editorial a few days after the vote.

> ". . . . . it is the duty of all who are good citizens of the community to accept that verdict whether or not they agree with it. If the Citizens' Association keeps alive to the needs of the town, there is much to be gained, although Smithers has progressed to the point where the local body has become impotent in dealing with the larger requirements of the community."

The matter of incorporation was raised periodically over the next seven months but it was not until early October, 1921, that the subject was again discussed at length. A slightly revised charter had arrived from Victoria but the real catalyst in re-opening the issue was the growing inability of volunteers to keep up with the work associated with running the community. In addition, the spectre of financial hardship had been somewhat banished by an announcement from the Province that one half of the proceeds from local liquor sales would now remain in the communities in which they were collected.

Accordingly, on October 21, 1921, the citizens of Smithers voted 169 to 54 in favour of

VICTORIA

Registered.

1 9 2 1
Sept. 27th

Hon. A. M. Manson,
PRINCE RUPERT, B.C.

Dear Sir:

In response to your telegram received this morning, I am forwarding herewith the Letters Patent for the incorporation of Smithers. Please look over these and return same as soon as convenient as this is the original and only copy of the Letters Patent on hand.

I am informed by the Attorney General's Department that in order to obviate the necessity for advertising the whole of these Letters Patent in the Gazette, a small amendment to the Village Incorporation Act will have to be passed at the forthcoming session.

I would particularly call your attention to Section 5 of the first part of this document. You will see that this provides for the appointment of three Commissioners by the Lieutenant-Governor in Council to carry on until the Municipal Council is elected. I would be pleased to have your advice in connection with these appointments.

Yours very truly,

John Oliver.

The 'Prime Minister' of the Province, the Hon. John Oliver agrees to the incorporation of Smithers as the first village in British Columbia under the "Village Incorporation Act."

J.R. McIntyre, G.T.P. Railway engineer and first Chairman of the Village Commissioners, 1921-23.

incorporation. Exactly one month later the articles patent arrived from Victoria making Smithers the first incorporated village in the Province. N.P. Moran, Charles Reid and J.R. McIntyre were appointed provisional commissioners pending the village's first municipal election.

In a somewhat guarded editorial, L.B. Warner congratulated the community on what was then considered a bold step in Smithers' progress.

> "Smithers is now declared a village under the Village Incorporation Act and the ship of state of this community emerges from the placid inland waters into the sea of the unknown . . . . . The responsibility placed upon the shoulders of the citizens of this town through incorporation will be a mighty factor in the progress of this place and if no further advantage is gained by the change, the experiment will have been justified and the community will be better off for the responsibility placed upon its people. Mistakes will be made in the first year. That is only natural and human. The Commissioners have no precedent to guide them, as this is the first village in the province, but there will be a willingness to overlook little slips on the recollection that some of the greatest triumphs were born in an error which preceded success."

When the ballots in the first election were counted on the evening of February 9, 1922, J.R. McIntyre, railroad engineer and a two-year resident of Smithers, had been elected mayor. N.P. Moran, proprietor of The Empress News Company, and George Wright, a conductor with the railway, had been elected to the two council seats, defeating aldermanic hopefuls Dr. C.H. Hankinson, Larry Warner and J.S. Kennedy.

CHAPTER 4

Before The Crash

The new Village Council soon familiarized itself with the ways of bureaucracy and addressed the priority of the day, a flow of cash into town hall. Within months by-laws were passed requiring the licencing of businesses, new buildings, dogs and automobiles. Tax bills were mailed out, liquor receipts collected and donations encouraged. At the end of the first year revenue amounted to $6,296.39 (including a $125.00 donation) against expenditures of $4,971.89. No deficit financing in those days! In addition to achieving a financial surplus in their first year of office, the Village fathers also attempted to enhance the urban nature of their community, first by outlawing the keeping of chickens within municipal boundaries and then by requiring that all horsedrawn vehicles be equipped with lights due to the frequency of collisions between them and the growing number of automobiles.

The years immediately following incorporation were, with the exception of the present, perhaps the most significant in the young community's pursuit of growth and sophistication. Messrs. McIntyre, Moran and Wright oversaw, during their two-year term of office, the installation of the Village's first telephone exchange, operated by Dominion Telegraph Co., a greatly expanded home electric service (from 9 to 11:30 on Tuesday mornings), and well over $100,000 in new construction, $75,000 of it in the first year. The local board of education petitioned the Village Council for land at Second Avenue and Columbia for construction of a new high school to replace the first high school on King Street at 3rd Avenue and the first appeals for a permanent provincial building (the Central Park Building) were being directed to Victoria. Hotel owners were appealing to Omineca M.L.A. A.M. Manson for the right to sell beer and liquor, a nurses residence was under construction on King Street, the first "undertaking parlour" was established by D.C. Sangster, and Fr. J. Allard, of the Roman Catholic Church, held the Village's first communion on Sunday, May 27, 1923.

Smithers' growing prominence on the northern map was not, however, common knowledge. The Vancouver Province, for instance, was quite unaware of it all, as evidenced by the following report from an August, 1922 edition of the paper.

> "Forest fires are reported in most of the country from Terrace to Burns Lake. In this country, however, there is little habitation. There are railway stations where lonely section crews of the G.T.P. make their homes and a settlement here and there. But forest fires in this area, if buildings escape, are likely to do more good than harm. Stunted jackpine and clumps of willows form the bulk of the timber. There is little or none that is merchantable."

Since the Province didn't know the G.T.P. had been taken over by the C.N.R. the year before, the paper's bold assertion of ignorance about B.C.'s first Village was not surprising. In any case, it did little to discourage one of the town's first

The power plant.

The elementary school at the corner of King and Third Avenue in 1937. Driver of the truck is Art Simpson. On the back of the truck are (L-R): Peter Small (hanging over the cab), Guy Ludgate, Bud Emerson, Bill Hann, Harry Kenney, Gordon Hetherington, Harold May, Marg Swift, May Roth, Marg Erickson, Ruth Anderson, Bill Leach.

~~VICTORIA~~

Prince Rupert, B.C., May 20, 1918.

Charles Reid, Esq.,
Secretary, Smithers Citizens' Association,
Smithers, B.C.

Dear Sir,-

I have yours of the 18th inst. I am glad that you got Mr Carruthers to go over the available buildings for Government Offices at Smithers. The reason that Mr Carruthers had no instructions I think was that Mr Hart, in whose Department this matter comes, went to Ottawa immediately after the session. He should be home in the course of a week or ten days and as soon as I hear of his being home I intend to wire him in connection with having this removal effected without delay.

As far as I am personally concerned, my attitude is shown by a letter which I wrote him on the 18th of March last, a copy of which I enclose, and which speaks for itself. I have supplemented this with a personal interview just before leaving Victoria and a letter to him since I came home.

Yours very truly,

AMM/M
Encl.

March 18, 1918.

Honorable John Hart,
Minister of Finance,
Victoria, B.C.

Dear Sir,-

I trust that in compiling the estimates you will not omit to provide for the transfer of the Government Agency from Hazelton to Smithers. We have promised this and the sooner the change is made the better for all concerned. The continuance of the agency in Hazelton makes needless trouble for me in that Hazelton is an unsatisfactory place and other points along the line are pressing hard to have the change made forthwith.

If the Government cannot see its way clear at the present time to build a new building at Smithers I would suggest a three year lease be taken on a building in Smithers which is at present available. The rental would be very nominal.

I am very anxious to see the change made. It simply must be made prior to the next election if this constituency is to remain Liberal and that being the case we may as well make it now. It is simply a thorn in the flesh for all concerned to have it remain in Hazelton.

Yours truly,

"A.M.Manson"

Much pressure was put on the Provincial Government to move government offices from Hazelton to Smithers. These efforts proved successful and construction on the Provincial Government building (now the Central Park Building) began in October, 1924.

residents and the man who was to guide Smithers' growth for the next six years.

E.E. (Ed) Orchard, owner of the Bulkley Hotel and Chairman of the Village Commissioners, 1924-27.

E.E. (Ed) Orchard, who succeeded J.R. McIntyre as mayor in February, 1924, was perhaps the community's first businessman. Following the announcement that Smithers would be a G.T.P. divisional point in 1914, Orchard established a restaurant and "rooms", all under canvas, for those who would survey the townsite and clear the land. In all, he had about 75 permanent boarders, plus transients, at this time. When the Bulkley Hotel was built a few years later, Orchard was hired as cook and eventually purchased the building in 1919 after leasing it for a year. His election as mayor in 1924 was but one of a number of civic contributions ranging from president of the Fall Fair Association and the local Automobile Club to chairman of the School Board and director of the Hospital Board.

Ed Orchard, as had his predecessors, was to witness and participate in his share of "firsts" in the community. In the same year that he won his municipal post, the provincial electoral district of Omineca was split into two parts. The Omineca seat was retained by incumbent A.M. Manson and the new Skeena riding was captured by pioneer physician Dr. H.C. Wrinch of Hazelton. One of Dr. Wrinch's first duties as an M.L.A. was to announce Victoria's intention to proceed with a provincial building for Smithers. Work on what we now refer to as the Central Park Building began in

The Pioneer Block. Constructed in 1926, it was shared for a number of years by Hanson Lumber and Timber Co., and the Royal Bank of Canada.It presently houses Apollo Automotive.

October, 1924. By July of the following year more than 100 foundation piles had been driven and by August the second storey was nearing completion. On January 29, 1926, the first court session was held in the new building and by March all government offices were housed in their new quarters. Other buildings which went up during the latter half of the decade included Olof Hanson's permanent office (now Apollo Automotive), the new high school (now Bulkley Valley Christian High) and Fred Watson's new general store at First Avenue and Main Street (Irly Bird Carpet Centre).

It was also during the 20's that two unique community industries flourished, Axel Anderson's brick works at Chicken Creek and the Lake Kathlyn ice harvest. Excessive freight rates had inhibited any kind of local market for bricks, despite their resistance to fire, but with the discovery of a high grade clay close to town, the future of the industry seemed guaranteed. Most of the actual plant building had been completed by July, 1928, and local merchant Fred Watson had already announced he would be the first to use the bricks in construction of his new store on Main Street. When production began, Anderson was turning out 1800 bricks an hour and soon upped that figure to 2,000. However, poor weather and mechanical problems seemed to plague the operation constantly. At one point, Anderson had to turn away almost $4,000 in orders, representing a dozen train car loads of bricks, due to operation problems.

The Lake Kathlyn ice harvest, while only seasonal, represented a major industry in the valley for years, providing temporary employment for many area residents. The two biggest customers were the C.N. Railway and Booth Fisheries in Prince Rupert. Beginning in January or February, when the ice reached a thickness of about two feet, the cutters would begin sawing out the frozen blocks. Production figures for 1924 show that 8,000 tons, or 400 train car loads, were shipped from the lakeside storage sheds that winter to Booth Fisheries. The C.N. contract called for between 5,000 and 7,000 additional tons.

Axel Anderson's Brick Works. The young boy on the left is Henry Anderson, a longtime Smithers resident until his death in 1979. Fourth from the left is Axel Anderson, owner of the brick works.

Axel Anderson's Brick Works near Chicken Creek, 1929.

The Lake Kathlyn ice harvest. Lake Kathlyn was named after the daughter of Sir Alfred Smithers. Prior to that time, it was called Chicken Lake after an Indian family by the name of Chicken who lived on the lake. The Indian people themselves called it "Boiling Lake." According to Indian legend, a huge fish inhabited the lake. It had a large appetite and one day ate the chief's beautiful daughter as she was fishing. This so angered the chief that he ordered his men to help him catch the fish, but the fish resisted all efforts to catch it. Finally, the chief and his men built a great fire to heat rocks which they then threw into the lake. When the lake reached the boiling point, the big fish was cooked right in the lake and died. Hence the name "Boiling Lake."

Local farmers claimed their share of advances during the 1920's as well, combining an ever deepening knowledge of their business with the prosperity of the times. With the announcement early in 1925 that a grain elevator would be constructed at the end of the C.N. rail line in Prince Rupert, area grain production increased dramatically. Wheat shipments out of the valley began very modestly in 1918, under the direction of F.M. Dockrill of Telkwa. By the late 20's, however, local farmers were shipping upwards of 1,000 tons annually and, according to the following Interior News report, the grain was of exceptional quality.

> "The first carload of wheat in the 1928 crop to be landed at Prince Rupert's elevator was from the crop harvested at the Chapman Ranch near Smithers. The grade certificate shows the carload as being No. 1 Northern, a high grade applying to practically all wheat being shipped from Smithers this year."

Timothy seed was another cash crop for local farmers who upped their production from 45 tons in 1925 to 275 tons in 1926, the year the Prince Rupert elevator began operation. Valley spud farmers, too, deserve credit, especially George Oulton, a Smithers dairyman who entered his seed potatoes in a 1924 competition with farmers from Idaho, the U.S. potato state. Oulton's production was double that of his southern competitors. Such was the interest in spuds locally that valley farmers formed a branch of the B.C. Certified Seed Potato Growers Association, headed by E.C. Barger, and adopted the slogan "Grown North of 53."

These too were lucrative years for the approximately 8,000 men involved in the Central Interior's forest industry. Statistics from the early to mid 20's indicate there were about 150 sawmills in the interior at this time with a daily capacity of 4-million feet and a payroll touching on $10-million. Not bad for an area which, according to the Vancouver Province, had no merchantable timber. Locally, in 1924, a new sawmill was established on the edge of Smithers. A.T. Harrer from Pennsylvania, B.F. Messner and his brother D.W. Messner, perhaps best known in more recent years for their involvement with a number of Babine mining properties, opened the lumber mill in August of that year. Situated just across the railway tracks off the water reservoir road, the mill had a daily production of 12,000 feet. Today one may find the remains of the old concrete foundations for the mill's steam boilers.

There was, needless to say, a substantial amount of cash changing hands in Smithers. Most of it was distributed in the course of daily commerce . . . but not all of it. At least $100 was exchanged at gunpoint in what may have been Smithers' first armed robbery. It began early on the morning of December 7, 1924, when a strongly built man, about 20 years old, registered at the Smithers Hotel (formerly The Dage) and soon after joined a game of Seven-Toed Pete, a variation of poker. According to the Interior News report, he lost a small sum of money before the game broke up, temporarily, while the players had breakfast. Before the game resumed, one of the participants took a roll of bills out of his pocket in order to repay a loan. The young man, later identified as Mike Sennuck of Prince Rupert, "whipped out a revolver with the command 'stick 'em up or you're dead men.' " He took $100 and, in the best western tradition, left by a rear door advising his former poker mates to remain inside for 15 minutes or he would "blow their heads off." He was captured later the same day in a search organized by Sergeant W.J. Service, head of the Provincial Police detachment in the district. Sennuck, with a record of offences in Saskatchewan and Ontario, pleaded guilty and was sentenced to five years in prison.

Five months later, the Smithers Hotel was the scene of another community milestone of sorts and a source of much celebration by local innkeepers. Their lobbying with M.L.A. Manson in Victoria had finally paid off with Editor Warner recording the event for posterity.

> "The Smithers Hotel opened up its emporium for the sale of beer by the glass on Saturday and the thirsty were on the ground early and late with their mouths as definitely open as the door of the first beer parlour in Smithers. The management has provided a very comfortable room."

The date was May 9, 1925, but unfortunately one of the community's more colourful citizens, and definitely a potential patron, was not on hand for the big event. J.S. (Kicker) Kelly, who had tried to unseat Attorney-General Manson in the 1920 provincial election, had come out second best again in his battles with the forces of law and order. In fact, he was doing six months in Oakalla Prison for the illegal possession of liquor, having lost an appeal on that conviction in November, 1924.

Liquor, too, played a part in an event of more tragic consequence, the Village's first auto fatality. During the last days of June, 1929, Uno Ferner and Issac Karlsen, passengers in a car driven by David Jones of Smithers, were killed when the car left the Duthie Mine Road. Jones was later charged with manslaughter, convicted, and sentenced to a year in prison.

Just two weeks later, another man, 27-year-old James Wesley Burke, was to achieve a degree of notoriety on the wrong side of the law by staging Smithers' first and, to date, only bank robbery.

What was to become a two-week manhunt began on the morning of July 17, 1929, when Burke, armed with a revolver, stole $2,000 from the Royal Bank at Main and Broadway, then fled across the railroad tracks and into the bush. L.H. Kenney, a local real estate agent and insurance salesman, gave chase and actually caught up with Burke. According to newspaper accounts of this exchange, Kenney told Burke he was free to go if he would only return the stolen money. Unfortunately, Kenney didn't know how much money Burke had taken. The man gave Kenney a wad of bills and headed into the bush once again, with the greater portion of the loot still in his possession.

L.H. Kenney, Chairman of the Village commissioners, 1936-37. Kenney gave chase to Smithers' only bank robber in 1929 and retrieved some of the stolen money.

Jack Joseph, Stephen H. Hoskins and Sgt. Corford after a successful fishing trip. Joseph was the Indian policeman who captured the bank robber.

During the course of the next week there were occasional reports from people who thought they may have seen Burke. In actual fact, he had somehow managed to get as far as Telkwa and buy food before anyone suspected who he was. It wasn't until Sunday, July 28, that J.R. McIntyre, Smithers' former mayor and an engineer with the C.N., spotted a man fitting Burke's description trying to steal aboard the eastbound passenger train near Walcott. Shortly thereafter he was captured by James Fairburn and Harry Holland and placed on a railroad speeder for transport back to Smithers. Near Quick, Burke grabbed a rifle and again escaped into the bush.

At this point Sergeant Service* organized a posse of 12 white men and three Indian trackers, Jack Joseph, Charley Thom and Patrick Charley. Reports on this portion of the manhunt maintain that the 12-member posse insisted on having breakfast before resuming the search. The three Indian trackers headed into the bush immediately upon arriving at Quick. They found Burke two miles away, asleep. "Jack Joseph took charge," according to the Interior News, "and kept the man covered with his rifle until delivered to the police." Authorities later recovered $1,150 from a cache near Walcott. Burke was convicted and sentenced to 10 lashes and five years in prison.

The population of Smithers, between 350 and 450 at the start of the 1920's, had reached 1,000 by mid-decade, a rate of increase which is perhaps only being equalled now. But while growth certainly characterized the decade, the community was not without its losses. Mrs. C.H. Hankinson, wife of the local doctor and daughter of undertaker D.C. Sangster, died in 1924 after a year-long illness. Only 29 at the time of her death, Mrs. Hankinson was survived by her husband and three children, the eldest being only four years old. Her father died two years later at the age of 57. As mentioned previously veteran prospector and mining man James Cronin died in 1925 after an 18-year association with the valley. T.T. (Tommy) Dunlop, district engineer with the Department of Public Works, died in 1924. A 15-year resident of the valley, Dunlop was killed when he fell into a swollen Bulkley River while inspecting the bridge pilings at the foot of Main Street. Obituaries were also written for Joseph H. (Jack) Hetherington who died in 1929 and for Gustav Rosenthal, former partner of L.L. Devoin in the Riverside Dairy.

As Smithers approached the end of the

*In July of 1938 Sgt. Service, who had risen to the rank of acting Inspector of the Provincial Police and was stationed in Prince Rupert, was shot to death by a man to whom he had issued a traffic ticket a few hours earlier.

The old Bulkley Bridge at the foot of Main Street was an important transportation link on Highway 16 for many years.

Shown on the bridge are Irma and Al Bannister with their Model T in the late 1920's. Granny Bannister is in the car.

decade, there was little to indicate the impending collapse of the North American economy. In mid-1928 the province, as a whole, experienced a slight drop in the value of mining stocks but this was written off as the inevitable result of almost a decade of growth in the industry, which is the subject of the next chapter.

Such had been the success of the previous 10 years that local businessmen, ironically anticipating more of the same, formed the Smithers Retail Merchants Association to promote local commerce. The inaugural meeting, held in January 1929, was conducted by President Fred Watson. That same year the community's Board of Trade decided to move itself up another notch, changing its name to the Chamber of Commerce. The promotion did not fail to catch the eye of one tongue-in-cheek southern columnist who was mightily impressed by the new name and said so in the following newspaper item.

> "Smithers, away up in Northern British Columbia, is putting on style. It means to get into the big-time city class along with London, Chicago and Buenos Aires. In the parlance of an earlier day, it is feeling its oats and is about to strut its stuff. The Smithers Board of Trade is changing its name! Henceforth it is to be known as the Chamber of Commerce.
>
> "So far as I can learn from my Canada Yearbook, Smithers will be the only town in the Dominion boasting a Chamber of Commerce. It may not hold the distinction long, but it will have it for a while anyway. That's what comes of being progressive, for Smithers has always been that."

The writer went on to say that not even Vancouver had a chamber of commerce but as soon as it got one it would "high hat Nanaimo and Chilliwack and Mission City even as Smithers will certainly high hat Endako and Kitwanga and Vanderhoof." As things turned out the following year, neither the Merchants Association nor the Chamber did much "high hatting" but there was at least one substantive bit of growth on the cultural front that was to transpire before the onset of the depression.

November of 1929 saw the birth of the Smithers Band, a cultural entity which, until only recently, played regularly throughout the valley and beyond. The bandmaster was jeweller J.S. Gray, with an executive consisting of H.G. Olsen, W.V. Tomlinson, A.C. Fowler and L.H. Kenney.

In so far as it is recorded in the Interior News, that was the last bit of good news the residents of Smithers were to have for a while. Reports of the stock market crash and its consequences filled the papers in succeeding weeks despite predictions of an imminent resurgence in the economy. So sure of this financial resurrection was local realtor L.H. Kenney that he purchased

The original Smithers Band, under the direction of John S. Gray, 1932. Front (L-R): John Gray, bandmaster, Tom Hetherington, Vernon Crockett (High school principal). 2nd row: L.H. Kenney, K. Collison, George Bowie, Harold Berg, H. Mathews, Percy Berg. 3rd row: Thor Hanson, Ole Fegsted, Don Collison, Reg Collison, Bill Doodson, Bill Collison. 4th row: Edgar Woodward, W. Tomlinson, Fred Wicks, Topsy Robinson, Bill Swift, Carl Raabe. Rear: Max Collison, Fred Fowler, Bill Grant, Dick Champion, Ernie Hann.

an ad, entitled "Big Slump In Stocks," in which he claimed "today's prices will look ridiculous within a few weeks" and counselled his clients to "buy heavily at the bottom of the bear market."

Few people, if any, were buying either Kenney's optimism or anything else. Railway tie orders dropped off by 50 per cent almost overnight, shutting down a number of tie camps. Credit became non-existent, U.S. tariff regulations were slapped on a number of commodities and bankruptcy announcements were frequent.

At about this same time residents of Smithers also learned that one of their urban pioneers and the man who had guided municipal growth during the latter half of the community's most prosperous decade was leaving. Forced by ill health to sell his Bulkley Hotel in 1929, Ed Orchard, Smithers' mayor since 1924, left with his wife and son for a new home in Bremmerton, Washington.

Coal Vein
near Lake Kathlyn
Killam
Smithers
B.C.

CHAPTER 5

Mining's Bright Decade

The next decade was a bleak one throughout North America and the residents of the Bulkley Valley were in no way immune to the economic malaise being experienced elsewhere. In fact, the Village's financial woes were but part of an apparent series of ill events which plagued the community during the early 1930s. Accidental deaths and injuries, fires and the like, all ostensibly unconnected with the Depression, formed the core of the news budget in the Interior News for quite some time after the stock market collapse. However, before dealing with these and other Depression era events, it is first necessary to deal with another aspect of the previous decade. If the 1920s had been boom years generally, they were particularly kind to members of the area mining fraternity. Reliable transportation, in the form of the C.N.R., and improved world markets produced great flurries of local mining activity which, at one point in 1925, saw development work proceeding on 25 valley properties. Another 18 had been identified as potential mine sites, depending on market conditions.

The most successful of all these ventures, in terms of production, employment and interest, was the Duthie Mine on the backside or southwest slope of Hudson Bay Mountain. Seattle shipbuilder J.F. Duthie acquired more than two dozen claims on the mountain, including the Mamie, Henderson and White Swan groups, during 1921 and 1922. First discovered just after the turn of the century, these properties had experienced little development due primarily to a shortage of capital by previous owners.

No such problems were encountered by Mr. Duthie who sank both money and tunnels into his claims almost immediately. Early in January 1923, his investment paid off with the discovery of a rich vein of silver on the Henderson property. By the end of that month two dozen workers, going day and night on three tunnels, had filled two railroad cars with ore destined for the smelter at Trail, B.C. By March there were reports of employees, in anticipation of break-up, trying to get enough rock down from the mine to fill the eighth ore car.

Duthie Mine overlooking Aldrich Lake, better known locally as Loon Lake.

Needless to say, Mr. Duthie possessed a very saleable commodity. His Henderson claim had proven ore reserves valued at about $175.00 a ton. In fact, Duthie had recovered the purchase price of the Henderson group by the end of 1923. The site was now equipped with permanent buildings and electric power and a road to the mine, started in April 1923, was well underway. Accordingly, he sold a controlling interest in the operation to the

The mine shaft at Duthie Mine.

Two vehicles meet on a narrow winter road at Duthie Mine on the back of Hudson Bay Mountain.

A 20-ton boiler being transported to Duthie Mine. Road conditions were sometimes less than ideal in the early days.

Federal Mining and Smelting Company, a division of the U.S. Guggenheim family of businesses, in July, 1923. Work continued with almost 1,000 tons of ore shipped by early 1924. However, in June of that year the new owners ceased all operations at the Duthie Mine, putting about 80 people out of work.

According to Federal Mining and Smelting Company officials, the shutdown was ordered because ore bodies had not held up as well as expected under development. Few observers, however, agreed, including L.B. Warner who offered his own unverified theory in the Interior News of July 2, 1924.

> "Reasons for the shutdown at the Duthie Mine are not so clear as they have been making regular shipments of very high grade ore since taking over management. It is well known that Mr. Duthie was far from satisfied with the work being carried on at the property and this came to a head at a conference in Seattle last week. With the notice received on Friday night to close down, opinions are held that such a move was not altogether voluntary."

It appeared, therefore, that a dissatisfied J.F. Duthie had somehow managed to wrest control away from Federal despite his minority share position. In any case local rumor had it that he would reopen the mine in the very near future, especially since most equipment had been left in place. It was a full year, however, before Duthie and the Guggenheims resolved their alleged dispute and resumed production. The mine reopened in July, 1925 and by November of that year 40 employees were producing 10 tons of ore daily with reserves in sight for another 18 months of work.

Production continued uninterrupted throughout 1926. At 1,242 tons shipped for the nine months ending September 30 that year, the Duthie Mine ranked ninth in production of all mines shipping to the Trail smelter. During 1927 Duthie installed his own ore mill and in October of that year a school was opened for children of mine employees. R.B. Wallace of Smithers was hired as teacher.

In February 1928, the Duthie Mining Company went public; putting 300,000 shares on the market, 50,000 of which were reserved for people living between Prince Rupert and Prince George. The offering was immediately oversubscribed and the value of the shares began to climb. Activity at the mine site paralleled that on the stock market as a new power generator was installed, doubling the production capacity. Reports put Duthie's net monthly profit at $20,000 in October, 1928, about the same time shareholders received their second dividend payment. By the end of 1928, the Duthie Mine was employing 45 men and producing 50 tons of ore daily.

The Guggenheims, in addition to their

The Duthie Mine. Shown here are Bob Andrews and Jim Bovill in the middle to late 1920's.

activities on Hudson Bay Mountain, were also active at a site about 30 miles east of Smithers. Dome Mountain, previously owned by the Jefferson Syndicate of New York, was acquired by the Federal Mining and Smelting Company in January, 1923. Development on the gold property began immediately. Camps were constructed, a power plant installed, tunnels built and trial shipments of ore sent out. Reports claimed the ore bodies, of which there were several, varied from a few inches up to many feet in width and were "remarkable in their length." However, at almost the same time as the Duthie shutdown, Federal closed down operations at Dome Mountain as well, again claiming ore deposits had not held up to expectations.

Ever vigilant to negative comments on the valley's mineral potential, Editor Warner offered a further explanation which may well have had application to the Duthie closure.

> ". . . while the general manager of the Federal Company blatantly peddles the yarn about the deposits being no good, there is the other statement by a still higher official that the withdrawal was no condemnation of the district but was forced by a decision of the head office (Wallace, Idaho) to close down all operations running on capital account owing to the unsettled conditions in Europe and in the Orient and all British Columbia operations were in a development stage operated on capital."

Warner went on to suggest that just because syndicates such as the Federal organization, which controlled 110 mining companies, were unwilling to risk their capital, valley ore bodies still warranted local investment. Better, he argued, to operate on a small scale using local capital than to shut down altogether. Some area businessmen, such as R.L. Gale, did respond to Warner's suggestion but never on a major level. As such, almost all mineral development was financed from south of the border.

The Duthie Mine was but one of several properties on Hudson Bay Mountain which saw extensive development during the 1920's. The Victory group, adjacent to the Duthie property, was another. Its proprietor, Donald C. Simpson, worked the property for about two decades earning, in the process, a reputation as one of Smithers' most hard-working, generous and opinionated citizens. Over the years Simpson put about 1,500 feet of tunnels into his property, sending out periodic ore shipments to the Trail smelter. He still found time, however, to write several letters to the Interior News. In one of these he attempted to place the credit for local mining development where he felt it belonged.

> "Due credit should be given to the moneyed operators of course, and more to that rare bird among mining engineers, the engineer who has mining vision and the courage to attempt the proving and realization of his conceptions, but it can be taken as an axiom that none of these ever yet put any mining district on the map until after that dauntless pioneer and explorer, the prospector, had shown and smoothed the way."

In addition to his letter writing, Simpson was also known for his generosity as he often hosted evening get-togethers for mining crews working on various Hudson Bay Mountain claims. The Victory Mine, never a big producer compared to the neighbouring Duthie property, was optioned along with another claim to Pennsylvania industrialist J.J. O'Brian in 1926 for $200,000.

Other Hudson Bay claims included the Amiens group, owned by R.L. Gale, the Empire group, also belonging to Donald Simpson, and Cascade, eight claims belonging to Alex S. Millar and M.E. LeBlanc of Seattle.

On the other side of the valley, in the Babine Mountains, another group of mining men had divided the landscape into about 15 groupings. Most noteworthy of these, in terms of eventual production, was the Babine Bonanza or what we now refer to as the Cronin Mine. James Cronin, who had already discovered two other mines in the provincie and put them into production, arrived in the Bulkley Valley in 1907, purchasing the Bonanza property in almost a raw state for $40,000. With the nearest railroad 700 miles away, the purchase was an obvious gamble although, by this time, word of the G.T.P.'s future plans was out. Cronin spent the next 16 years and about $200,000 of his own money developing the Bonanza property. In addition, the provincial government put up $30,000 for a winter road into the site. By 1923 Cronin had blocked out what he estimated were 50,000 tons of ore averaging about $30 a ton. With $1.5 million of ore in sight, Cronin packed up in October and headed south for the winter anticipating the start of actual production in the spring. On his way down from the property, he was seriously injured when his horse stumbled and fell. He died in 1925 as a result of the injury and it was not until 1928 that operations resumed at the mine site.

The new owners, Babine Bonanza Metals Ltd., spent another year developing the property for Eastern Canadian interests. Government assays showed the ore contained 1.42 ounces of gold and 440 ounces of silver per ton. Then, as the property neared the actual production stage for the second time, the stock market collapsed as did the market value of silver.

The Babine Bonanza Mine was but one of several properties that were actively worked, both physically and on the stock market, during the 1920's. Most important of these were the six-claim Victoria group, Silver King, Little Joe, Hyland Basin and Silver Saddle. All of these properties were worked over the years by a variety of men whose names became synonymous with Babine Mountain mineral exploration. P.J. (Paddy) Higgins, B.F. Messner, D.W. Messner, A.T. Harrer, Tommy King, Martin Cain and Axel Elmsted spent most of each year either working or promoting these properties. In August, 1926, the Messners and A.T. Harrer, owners of the Silver Saddle group, amalgamated the properties. Silver King was bonded to the new organization by owner J. Ginsmer, as was the Victoria group, owned by Paddy Higgins, and Little Joe and Hyland Basin, owned by Cain and King.

At various times ore shipments were made from all of these properties but they never attained the kind of production that would qualify them as actual mines. The Victoria group, known later as Native Mines, received substantial backing from Seattle and Vancouver interests early in 1929, but again the onset of the depression put an abrupt end to promises of production.

Access to all of these claims, at least from the western side of the Babine Range, was gained via a trail paralleling Driftwood Creek. It was along this trail that another of Smithers' mining men made both his home and his living.

C.G. (Peavine) Harvey, a veteran prospector even before his arrival in the valley in 1907, came to Smithers in 1914 after a seven-year stint as a hotel operator in Hazelton. Bringing his six-month

The Cronin Mine in later years (mid 1950's).

C.G. (Peavine) Harvey. Photo by Bill Davidson, a constable of the B.C. Provincial Police. circa 1939.

This is believed to be tunnel no. 1 on the Big Onion mountain in the Babines. L-R: Oscar Lundstrom, Axel Elmsted, Duncan Jennings. Jennings later bought the Broughton and McNeil store at Lake Kathlyn, renaming it Jennings store.

Well-known mining figures L-R: Axel Elmsted, Henry Messner, Harry Clement, Frank Messner and Ben Mueller in front of the cookhouse, Cronin Mine.

old son and wife with him, Peavine settled on what is now Driftwood Road, but spent much of his time working a mineral claim on the western face of the mountain which now bears his name. About 50 years old when he arrived in Smithers, Peavine continued working his property well into his eighties, making occasional shipments of ore, some of which returned a little over $100.00 a ton. Most of his production was accomplished with the bare essentials - hand drill, shovel and wheelbarrow. Characterized by a booming voice (which some claim carried the length of Main Street) and his pride (occasionally mistaken for stubborness), Harvey also fancied himself a farmer, this pursuit giving rise to the acquisition of his nickname. According to a written account of the affair provided by his son Gordon, who died in 1977, Peavine had prepared some exhibits for the Pacific National Exhibition (P.N.E.) in Vancouver.

> "Included was a sheaf of our famous timothy hay and some wild huckleberries. The night before he left, some 'friends' stole into his hotel room and made some changes. In place of timothy, they put a bundle of local peavine hay and replaced the berries with a box of rabbit manure. He didn't discover it until he arrived at the P.N.E. in Vancouver."

Mr. Harvey's frustrations must have been considerable but in terms of his nickname, he could have done worse.

Peavine Harvey died in 1945 at the age of 90.

One of Peavine's mining associates, and a man of no less determination, was the aforementioned "Kicker" Kelly. Already a two-time loser in his encounters with men of the law, Kelly did manage to "get one back" towards the end of the 1920's. Taking aim at the imposing figure of J.F. Duthie, Kelly charged the Duthie Mining Company with stealing $5,000 worth of equipment from him. Several months later, the case was settled out of court, Kelly receiving $600 and costs.

Aside from the Duthie and Cronin mines, and the Goat Creek coal deposits near Telkwa, all of which are still being modestly worked today, Smithers' area mineral deposits have yet to see the degree of development witnessed during the 1920s. There was a resurgence of activity during the mid-1960s centred primarily on copper and molybdenum. But in terms of the old and once promising gold, silver, lead and zinc claims, little has transpired since the 1929 Wall Street crash. Perhaps much of the optimism of the 20s can be attributed to a significantly inferior knowledge of geology in comparison with todays standards. In other words, we now have a much clearer understanding of the quality and quantity of the deposits and their relevance in the market place. Late in 1929, however, many readers of the Interior News would have liked to agree and perhaps did agree with L.B. Warner's assessment of the situation, its implications for the valley's mining future, and what should be done to remedy that situation.

> "Newspaper headlines may have shrieked 'Billions Lost On Wall Street' but of course the stocks that were sold, like those that were kept, are worth just as much today as they were before the cyclone. Some of them may be worth more. Chalkmarks on a blackboard don't make values; they merely represent prices. The tickers tell not what a stock is worth but what somebody is willing to pay for it. Now that the speculative orgy on the stock market has resulted in the inevitable collapse, it may be a little easier to interest the public in placing surplus funds in development enterprises - where the money, even if no 'safer', will help build up the country and thus accomplish a public benefit."

Unfortunately, there wasn't much of a surplus around.

Nonetheless, the "engineers with vision" and the prospectors had contributed a very large share to the commerce and character of the Smithers of the 1920's. Men of the wilderness, for the most part, and unencumbered by social convention, their presence brought a freshness to a community bent on conforming to the patterns of urban development.

SMITHERS B.C. DEC 1927.

CHAPTER 6

The Thirties: Life on $2.80 A Day

At the outset of the Depression few people could anticipate just how bad things were going to be. The most optimistic of the seers claimed the economic hardships would be of short duration and would have a cleansing effect on the commerce of the nation. L. B. Warner was one of these.

In an editorial headed "Facing Another New Year", published on January 1, 1930, Warner said conditions since the stock market crash "are reaching a point where there are better times in sight."

> "Perhaps the experience of the past few months will be good for us all; the whole world may profit from the mistakes of the past and their success of the future may be all the greater because of a lesson learned so painfully and at such a price. Possibly thousands will be better off because they have learned a lesson in natural laws."

The better times were an illusion and if lessons had been learned, their application was not to be felt for some years. Local economic deterioration began almost immediately. Within days of the market collapse on Wall Street and in other financial centres, large orders placed by eastern and U.S. customers with the George Little Lumber Company and the Hanson Lumber and Timber Company were cancelled. In Hanson's case, the cancellation shut down all of his woods operations and left 100,000 poles backlogged in supply yards. Orders for railway ties from the Hanson company dropped from 150,000 in 1929 to 10,000 in 1930 with similar decreases affecting other contractors.

Olof Hanson, founder of the Hanson Lumber and Timber Company. He supplied ties to the G.T.P. Railway during its construction and then expanded into cedar pole and log supply to the United States. His operations extended from Prince Rupert to Endako, his headquarters being in the Pioneer Block, corner of Main and Broadway, in Smithers. Mr. Hanson also served as M.P. for Skeena for 16 years. He died in 1952.

Two versions of the Depression "Bennett Buggy" — a summer model (completely convertible), and an enclosed winter model. As the Depression deepened and gasoline became harder to get, this form of transportation became more popular. Made of cars or parts of cars, the "Bennett Buggies" got their name from Richard Bedford Bennett — the man who had the misfortune of being Canada's Prime Minister during the worst years of the Depression from 1930 to 1935.

The man in the upper photograph is Charlie Neal.

Early in February, 1930, the Duthie Mining Company shut down its milling and shipping operations in response to market conditions. Two weeks later all operations at the mine were halted, putting over 100 employees out of work. The mine remained idle until 1939 when A. W. Kelly and J. J. Herman obtained a working option on the property.

Other local indicators of financial hardship saw the hospital in hot water with local merchants for not paying its bills, The Interior News was reduced from eight to four pages and the 1933 Fall

Fair was cancelled due to lack of funds.

As the Depression deepened, the number of fires in the district seemed in increase dramatically. Early in June, 1930, several buildings, with a total value of $30,000, were lost in Telkwa while most of the community's citizens were at a Round Lake picnic. A few weeks later, the Hudson Bay Lumber Company mill in Smithers, operated by D.W. Messner, burned to the ground with losses estimated at $25,000. On January 3, 1931, fire severely damaged Sargent's Store in Smithers. For owner R.S. Sargent, business conditions didn't warrant repairing the structure. He left, ending an 18-year association with the community. Three months later, the business section of Hazelton was gutted with the loss of the Omineca Hotel, two cafes and a garage. In November, four buildings, all belonging to R.S. Sargent in Hazelton burned to the ground. Six Burns Lake businesses were lost to fire in May, 1931. And in April, 1933, the Smithers Hotel, known as the Dage when built a decade before, was levelled.

Adding to the general gloominess of the Depression decade was the passing of a number of the village's best known citizens. L.L. Devoin, of the Riverside Dairy died late in 1930, a victim of bronchial pneumonia. The early years of his quarter century in the valley had been spent in partnership with Joe Coyle at The Omineca Herald in Hazelton.

Smithers' grocer, Fred Watson, died in 1936 at the age of 51. A native of England, he emigrated to Utah when he was 12 years old, about 1896, and worked at a range of jobs from mining and farming to driving a stage-coach. He left the U.S. in 1909, arriving in Prince Rupert where he worked briefly for the railroad before landing a job in the grocery business. He arrived in Smithers about the same time as the rail line, married the community's first school teacher, Miss Mary K. Downey, and went to work for grocer H.F. Noel. In 1917, he enlisted for overseas service but was back in Smithers in 1919

Despite the gloom of the Depression, there were many good times. Shown here is the Royal Canadian Legion Hall on Broadway, all decked out to celebrate the coronation of King George VI on May 12, 1937.

Love, too, was not forgotten during the Depression. Here are Mr. and Mrs. Carl Mortensen on their wedding day, October 5, 1936. Mortensen was Regional District representative for many years. He died in 1980.

working for a short while for R.S. Sargent before going into business for himself. He eventually constructed his own grocery store at First and Main. An early member of the Citizens Association, and later the Chamber of Commerce, Fred Watson was also active in establishing the first hospital in the community and the first Fall Fair. When he died in July, 1936, he left behind his wife, five sons and a daughter.

Late in October, 1939, Dr. Horace Cooper Wrinch died at his home in Vancouver after serving the Bulkley Valley as physician and M.L.A. for almost 40 years. Born in England, Dr. Wrinch received his medical training in Toronto before coming to British Columbia in 1889 as a medical missionary for the Methodist Church. He was stationed first at Port Essington but soon moved to Kispiox and later to Hazelton where he turned his home into a hospital. In writing Dr. Wrinch's obituary, L.B. Warner had this to say of the man.

> "In the truest sense of the term he was a 'horse and buggy' doctor. It was nothing for him to ride saddle for the 200 miles over trail from Hazelton to the Ootsa Lake country to render service to those afflicted. It was this self-punishment and kindness that endeared him to the hundreds of early pioneers who remain to regret his passing."

Dr. Wrinch was elected to the provincial legislature twice, once in 1924 and again in 1928. In 1936, he severed his relationship with the valley, moving to Toronto, but returned to B.C. the following year to make his home in Vancouver. He was 74 at the time of his death.

Other prominent members of the community who passed away between 1930 and 1940 included Alexander Chisholm, former hardware store owner, and J. Mason Adams, the village's

Dr. H.C. Wrinch.

Asa Robinson and his daughter Betty with a days catch on the set line. A set line was a set of poles with fishing lines attached to them. The lines were left dangling in the river and checked usually once a day to see what had been caught. It was a popular way to ease the grocery bill during the Depression.

pioneer druggist who succumbed to cancer in California in 1937. Simon Gunannoot of Hazelton, who had eluded police for 13 years after being charged with murder in 1906, died on his trapline in 1933.* Prospectors Donald Simpson, who had discovered his Victory Group on Hudson Bay Mountain in 1906, and Martin Cain, one time owner of the Little Joe claim in the Babines, both died towards the end of the decade. Cain died when he lost his way during a winter trip into the Little Joe property. Glentanna ranchers Charlie Chapman, a former associate of James Cronin, and Charles A. Newitt, a 30-year resident of the valley and a veteran of the Riel Rebellion, also died during the Depression. And finally, J.C.K. Sealy, valley rancher, hotel owner, butcher and former pack train operator, died in 1940 at the age of 74.

The early years of the Depression were the hardest and it was during this time that the provincial government made some attempts at helping the estimated 400 unemployed in the district. Road construction was the focus of the relief efforts as the government spent thousands of dollars establishing work camps between Prince Rupert and Prince George. In August 1931, notices were posted around the village calling for registration of the unemployed "in order that they may be assembled in the camps for the carrying on of authorized works in an orderly manner." However, in November of the same year, several of these camps were shut down, apparently without explanation, and the workers sent home. According to newspaper reports of this time, the camps provided little relief even when they were operating. Single men who did manage to land a job in one of them were paid $7.50 a month. Their married counterparts, separated from their families, earned $2.80 a day. In addition, few of these men worked for more than two or three days at a time before being laid off as part of the rotation system on which the camps operated.

In view of all this, it is surprising just how much was accomplished during the decade. In terms of the day-to-day life of the village, Ernie Hann and H.J. Windt, acting fire marshalls, presided over acquisition of the first fire truck. The Smithers Golf Course was opened officially at 2:30 p.m. May 16, 1931 with Charles Reid as president of the six-hole circuit. The airport runway was constructed in the Tatlow road area the same year and in 1933, Oswald Hoskins, formerly of Henry Motors, opened his own garage at the corner of Main and Fifth Avenue, now Highway 16.

In February 1935, the village's own Chris

*Gunanoot gave himself up to the police in 1919 and was subsequently acquitted on the charge against him.

The Columbia Power Commission power house at Alfred and Manitoba streets in the 1930's.

Golf tournament, 1935. L-R: Bob Davidson, President of the Club enjoying a victory drink, Frank Dockrill, __________, Len Evans (standing), Chuck Cousins (seated), Jeff Woodall and L.G. Calder.

Hoskins Garage at the corner of Main and Highway 16.

Chris Dahlie, Western Canada Championships, Smithers in 1935. Dahlie was both jumping and cross country champion.

Dahlie capped a magnificent ski jumping career by winning the Western Canadian Ski Championship competition held that year in Smithers. Pitted against national contestants, Dahlie outscored them all in the combined 18-kilometer race and Class A jumping events and then retired. He later turned down an invitation to compete in the 1936 Olympics in Germany.

Later in the decade new settlement patterns began evolving with the arrival of the L'Orsa, Tugnum and Gyger families, as well as Joe Wettstein, M. Dettwiler and the Muheims, all originally from Switzerland.

The actual population of the village at the outset of the Depression, while well over 1,000 by most counts, was listed by the Federal Bureau of Statistics as 999. That same government office also provided a breakdown of the community's population according to the origins of its citizens.

English	— 339	Hebrew	— 1
Irish	— 154	Italian	— 1
Scottish	— 223	Polish	— 14
French	— 43	Roumanian	— 1
Czeck	— 1	Russian	— 3
Dutch	— 17	Ukrainian	— 6
Scandinavian	— 130	Asian	— 25
German	— 18	Other	— 25

Whatever its dimensions and origins, the village's population by 1933 was exerting a tremendous strain on a number of the community's original buildings. Foremost among these was a two-storey structure on King Street

Swiss immigrants headed for Smithers aboard the Cunard liner "Ascania" in April 1937. Front (L-R): A Waffler boy, Bill Gyger, John Gyger, another Waffler boy. 2nd row: Rosa Hug, Ida Hug, Marie Gyger, Emma Gyger, Agnes Schibli, Fritz Gyger Sr. 3rd row: Mrs. Gyger, Mrs. Waffler, Mrs. A. Schibli, Mrs. Hug. 4th row: Mr. J. Schibli, a steward holding the Waffler girl, Ben Hug, John Schibli, Louis Schibli, Ernest Michel. Rear: Deck hand, Martin Muntwiler, Josef Wettstein, Fritz Gyger, Mr. B. Hug. Missing from the group are Mr. Waffler and Ernest Hug.

The Bulkley Valley District Hospital, 1934.

The Sisters of St. Ann who ran the Bulkley Valley District Hospital from its opening in 1934 until 1969. Their service to the community has not gone unnoticed and has been appreciated by residents of the entire valley.

which, since 1920, had served as the Smithers hospital. Formerly a private residence, the building provided between 12 and 15 beds and, according to a brief history of hospital care in Smithers prepared recently by Bulkley Valley District Hospital personnel, was staffed by Dr. Hankinson, three nurses, a cook and a handyman.

> "The latter had the title of 'engineer,' probably due to his ability to keep a decrepit lighting plant in operation when he was not stoking stoves or exterminating rats!"

The need for a new hospital was obvious but where to find the necessary construction funds was not. The existing hospital board appealed through Bishop E. M. Bunoz in Prince Rupert, to a Victoria-based order of nuns. The Sisters of St. Ann, already involved in the provision of health care in the provincial capital, agreed to take over management of the new Smithers hospital which, according to original estimates, would cost about $24,000 to build. The expense was to be shared equally among the sisters, the village and the province. However, the sisters took an active hand in drawing up the plans and when they were finished the new estimate was closer to $60,000. The difference between the original estimate and the actual cost was covered by the sisters.

Located on the site of today's Bulkley Valley District Hospital, the 45-bed structure was completed in February, 1934, and was officially opened four months later. In attendence were Bishop Bunoz, Provincial Architect H. Whittaker, health ministry officials, Skeena M.L.A. E.T. Kenney and Frank Dockrill, representing Telkwa. Also attending were J.W. Turner, chairman of the hospital board, Charles Morris, representing the Village of Smithers and officials from the order of the Sisters of St. Ann. An addition, known as the Memorial Wing, was constructed in 1955, increasing the number of beds from 45 to 63, and in 1969 the Sisters of St. Ann returned the ownership and operation of the hospital to the community through the B.V.D. Hospital Society.

The Experimental Farm.

The Telkwa Creamery, circa 1939. B.C. Provincial Archives photo.

Another of the valley's major landmarks had its beginning during the Depression decade as well. Years of petitioning by the Board of Trade, the Chamber of Commerce and farmer's organizations finally paid off in June 1936 with the announcement from Ottawa that an "experimental farm or model farm" would be established somewhere in the Skeena electoral district. It was more than a year later that the following article was carried in the Interior News.

> "After investigating many places in the valley, officials of the Dominion Department of Agriculture have definitely selected the W. Sproule ranch for the experimental farm to be established in this district. Centrally located about midway between Telkwa and Smithers, on the main highway, the site is considered to be an excellent one for the purpose, the investigation showing it to be highly representative of the soils in a wide area the farm will serve.
>
> It is understood that work is to start early next month [August 1937] on further development of the farm.
>
> The government got a real bargain in the deal. There is something like 180 acres in the place and there is a large acreage now in crop. There are also good buildings. The purchase price was only $5,500 and this includes the crop."

Actual construction work on the experimental farm began late in 1938 when Ernie Hann supervised erection of a new residence, general purpose barn, implement shed and poultry house. Now known as the Northern Training Centre, the property was taken over by the provincial government about a decade ago.

Further east, in Telkwa, another grand opening was to mark the growing prosperity so much in evidence during the latter years of the decade. Alfred Miller, owner of the Interior Creamery in Prince George, opened his new $10,000 Telkwa Creamery May 12, 1939. The plant, capable of producing 1,000 pounds of butter daily, served cream producers from Burns Lake to Hazelton for the next several years.

While devoting most of his news columns to the economic resurgence of the valley during 1938 and 1939, L.B. Warner also indulged in what must have been a particular weakness for the athletic endeavours of his community. What were often lead stories on Page One of The Interior News carried headlines such as SMITHERS PUCKSTERS SHOWER PRINCE GEORGE WITH RUBBER or SMITHERS WON PUCK SERIES IN TILTS AGAINST PRINCE GEORGE. The 1939 team that

The Smithers Junior Hockey Champions, 1940-41. Front (L-R): G. Hetherington, M.McIntyre, P. Mayer, L. Warner, B. Hann. Standing: B. Leach, B. O'Neill, N. Kilpatrick, G. Ludgate, B. Washbern, Walter Watson, C. Steele (coach).

The Smithers Senior Hockey team, circa 1940. Front (L-R): Doug Kerr, Jack Hetherington, Jack Chapman, John Dunlop. Rear: Harley Lewis, Cliff Warner (coach), Bob Dunlop, Wilf Abel, Mel McIntyre, Mike O'Neill, Wilf Watson, Jack McEwen (manager).

Jim Davidson (left) and Joe Kelly (right) on the outdoor skating rink at King and First Avenue.

A hockey face-off in the 1930's. L-R: Cecil Steele, Ken Warner (referee), and Len Evans. The original curling rink, scene of many an exciting competition, is in the background.

regularly humiliated the Prince George squad consisted of, among others, Jack Dunlop, Bob Dunlop, Pete Mayer, Fred Watson (Jr.), Paul Raymond, Mel McIntyre, J. Hetherington, Billy O'Neill, G. Ludgate, Billy Leach, T. Hetherington, G. Hetherington, Bill Beaton, W. Abel, J. Chapman and H. Lewis.

Competing for first page space with the hockey players were Smithers curlers. Great detail was provided for readers in such stories as

KEWEN'S TWISTERS GET HANSON MUG which ran in the February 1, 1939 issue of the paper. Skips in that particular contest, listed in order of their finish, were J.L. McEwen, Art Simpson, J.G Stephens, W. Carey, R.C. Davidson, Wm. Duff, Frank Johnson, J.P. Downey, R.C. Bamford, W.J. O'Neill, P. Davidson and L.H. Kenney.

The village, by 1939, was a quarter of a century old and, as such, there were numerous anniversaries celebrated. One of these, particularly noteworthy in as much as the business is still going strong today, was that of the Smithers Lumber Co. Founded as the Williams-Carr Lumber Company in 1913, the business was taken over in 1914 by the founder of Terrace, George Little. During Mr. Little's ownership there was a succession of managers including E.T. Kenney, T.A. McMartin and Ernie Hann. In 1927, A.C. Fowler took over the manager's post and, in 1936, bought the operation in partnership with R.J. Collison. Located at the corner of Queen and Alfred from its beginnings, Smithers Lumber Yard moved to its Highway 16 access road location in 1972.

The year previous, in 1938, two other anniver-

Another popular sport was basketball. The Smithers High School girls were basketball champs in 1933. Rear (L-R): Helen Mehaffey, Della Carpenter (now Della Herman), Pat Hetherington,Kath Giraud (now Kath Gordon). Front: Mertyle McIntyre, Bea Monks (now Bea Leach) and Winnie Hann (now Winnie Robinson).

Boys High School basketball team, 1930's. Rear(L-R): Vernon Crockett (principal), Ken Warner, Stu McLeod, Len Evans, Harley Lewis, Mel Kerr. Front: Dan Foster, John Dunlop, Mike O'Neill. As the team could not afford proper uniforms, the jerseys were borrowed from the soccer team.

Boys High school baseball team, 1931. Rear (L-R): Joe Watson, John Carpenter, Vernon Crocket (principal and sponsor of the team), Jack Furness, Ernie Kershaw (teacher and coach). Centre: Angus McLean, Wilf Watson, Pat Carr, Len Evans. Front: Bob Chisholm, Pat Downey, Bill Leach (mascot), Jack Chapman, John Dunlop.

Smithers Lumber Yard at the corner of Alfred and Queen. First known as the Williams-Carr Lumber Co., it was later called Coast Lumber Co. before assuming its present name. The business was relocated to Highway 16 East in 1972.

A.C. "Fred" Fowler (left) and Reg Collison (right) co-owners of the Smithers Lumber Yard. Fowler bought out the partnership in 1951. Fowler was an extremely active man for the community. He was President of the Chamber of Commerce, elected to Village Council in 1951, and served as Chairman of the Council from 1952 to 1963. He was active in the St. James Anglican Church, and received the "Good Citizen" award in 1951. He was the first freeman of the Town of Smithers. The Pacific North West Hockey League trophy, the "Fowler Cup," is named after him. He died in 1974 at the ripe old age of 85, having lived a full life.

saries were celebrated. Twenty years had passed since the end of World War One and L.B. Warner, at the age of 51, was embarking on his third decade as publisher of The Interior News. Two years later, on February 27, 1940, he died, the victim of a heart attack.

Born in Brentwood, Ontario, Mr. Warner learned the printing trade with The Barrie Examiner and The Welland Telegraph, two Ontario newspapers. In 1910, he joined the staff of the Prince Rupert Daily Optimist and the next year he was married. He later moved to New Hazelton where he worked with Joe Coyle on The Omineca Herald before coming to Smithers in 1918 as publisher of The Interior News.

During his 22 years in Smithers, Larry Warner affected almost every aspect of community life as evidenced in the following biography, prepared by his son Ken.

"L.B. 'Larry' Warner was publisher of the Smithers Interior News from April, 1918, till his passing in February, 1940. He was active in every community endeavour from the moment he arrived here. He became active in the Citizens Association of the new community and was appointed to the executive of the organization in 1918. That same year he was appointed to the School Board as Chairman, Secretary in 1923 and a trustee in 1931 and '32.

" 'L.B.' was involved in negotiations with the provincial government for incorporation of the community in the early '20s which met with success in 1921. He was elected to the Village Council and served one term as Chairman in 1930-31. During these early years he was also active as a member of the Hospital Board, culminating in the goal of seeing the new hospital constructed and opened in 1934, operated by the Sisters of St. Ann.

"Along with other early pioneers of the community 'L.B.' was involved in establishing the Bulkley Valley Fall Fair at the former site on the Civic Centre grounds. He took over duties as first secretary of the Fair, a position he held until 1923, when he was honored by members of the association with the gift of a gold watch, locket and chain in recognition of his contribution.

"He was instrumental in the formation of the Associated Boards of Trade of Central B.C., being elected President of the association for two terms as well as being active on the local Board. He was prominent in organizing a local branch of the Native Sons of Canada, serving as President and in other offices. He was appointed the first Justice of the Peace for the community in 1927, a commission he resigned in 1931."

Main Street in the late 1930's.

A celebration to close off the decade — Klondike Days, 1939. Front (L-R): Fay Gamblin, Jim Silver, Tony Sartori, Joe Watson, Oswald Hoskins. Centre: Wilf Watson, Herb Leach, Al McKinnon, Mel Raymond, Pete Eby. Rear: Fred Watson, Jack McDonnell, Jack Dando, Wiggs O'Neill, Ralph Smith, Charlie Morris, Jim Downey, Clary Goodacre.

A Soldier's Farewell, World War II.

In the two years between his twentieth anniversary as publisher and his passing, Larry Warner was to record the onset of World War Two and its effects on the community. Among the first to enlist were Bill Collison, Alfred Howell, Graham Collison, Jiggs Graham, Larry Warner Jr., Mike O'Neill, Stan Heavysides and Cecil Ebert. Before their marching orders arrived however, three of these men were married, all within three days of one another. News of the unions was reported late in December as Michael Clarence O'Neill married Gweneth Louise Washbern, Graham Pinter Collison wed Ruth Rosalie Seely daughter of Jim Seely, and William H. M. Collison married Olive Barbara Evitt.

For some local ladies, however, marriage was the last thing on their minds, according to a story which appeared late in 1939.

> "Ladies of Smithers show every emotion from wrath and indignation to an overpowering patriotism in their willingness to take any part assigned to them.
>
> "In the past week these young ladies have learned more concerning the geography of Europe than they did in all the school days, and just let any loving lizard try to listen to a love song over the radio when the war news was on! They are frantically anxious to get someplace where they can do something about Europe's bad man of 1939. They don't see where they can do anything about it in Smithers."

Within the agricultural community, a special request was being made by District Agriculturist S.G. Preston. He advised valley farmers to leave grain production to their prairie counterparts and concentrate on beef and dairy cattle, sheep and hogs. Any locally produced grain, suggested Preston, should be used to fatten the hogs as meat was a prized commodity overseas.

Bill Morris, now one of the valley's best known ranchers, was involved in another line of work when the war broke out . . . but he too was simply awaiting the call, according to the Interior News.

> "William Morris returned to Smithers this morning, having spent the season as a fish buyer at Prince Rupert. It is eloquent of the success Bill achieved to say he brought back the first ten-dollar bill the editor has seen for some time — and flattered us by asking us to make the change. Bill will be in Smithers until such time as he is called to service in the navy."

As the Depression decade ended, the war effort began to materialize in earnest. New taxes were imposed on a variety of services and commodities from electricity to beer. Red Cross chapters were reactivated, investing much of their time in fund raising, and visits from recruiting officers were a regular occurence. Local volunteers often began their service in home defence with the 2nd Searchlight Division and 102nd Artillery Battalion in Prince Rupert. A number of them were then transferred overseas.

Promotion of War Savings Stamps for World War II. The young boy with his hand in front of his face could not be identified. The others are, l-r: Jim Seely, Ken "Kingfish" Collison, Fred Fowler, Bill Bovill, Slim Goodacre, Jim Bovill, Charley Morris, Max Collison and Harley Lewis.

CHAPTER 7

The War Years And Beyond

Smithers, as did most communities in Canada, underwent a number of war-related changes. Some, such as food and fuel rationing, occasioned a degree of sacrifice and hardship but they were transitory. Of a more lasting nature, however, was the acceleration of work on road and air links between Smithers and other provincial centres.

The need for reliable transportation routes, as part of an effective home-defence program, led to a major federal government announcement early in 1942. Work was to begin immediately on a military road linking Prince Rupert with Hazelton, thereby giving interior communities their first road access to the coast.

Surveys were underway by March of that year and by June most of the contracts for the Prince Rupert to Terrace section had been awarded, the majority of them going to Toronto-based companies. Two years later, in July of 1944, the road span across some of the most difficult terrain in all of Canada was nearing completion. However, the expense had been enormous, prompting Ottawa to approach Victoria for financial help in finishing the undertaking. The Province washed its hands of any responsibility for the project, a position which earned Victoria the following editorial rebuff in The Interior News.

> "It is hard to understand the government's attitude since the province has been more than a little fortunate in having a road completed from Kitwanga to Prince Rupert, a job which would probably have taken another century at the rate the province was going before the war."

Nonetheless the highway was completed a few months later, though the cost was never mentioned due to war time censorship regulations. About 250 guests attended the opening ceremonies, held September 4, 1944, in Terrace. Constructed primarily for military purposes, no one, especially the people of Prince Rupert, failed to recognize the long-term benefits of the new road. A half-page advertisement, addressed to "the citizens of Smithers, Telkwa, Burns Lake and Fraser Lake" and paid for by Prince Rupert interests stated:

> "The opening of this highway gate between Prince George — The Hub of The North — and The Sunset Port of Prince Rupert is the greatest development stimulus since the railway was carved through 30 years ago.
> "It will serve to unite the entire Northland, as nothing else could, and will create an active, neighbourly spirit that will bring this vast country — with its tremendously rich but greatly undeveloped timber, mining and farming land — into its own.
> "It will mean thousands of tourist dollars for this part of the province, bringing to realization a dream held throughout the years by SMITHERS, TELKWA, BURNS LAKE, FRASER LAKE and PRINCE RUPERT and all other communities in this vast and potentially wealthy empire of Northern British Columbia."

In the year prior to Ottawa's announcement of a "military" highway, reports began circulating that the Smithers area might be considered as a

The opening of Highway 16, linking Hazelton to Prince Rupert. The ceremony was held in Terrace on September 4, 1944.

possible site for a Department of Transport airfield, one of several that would link the prairies, B.C.'s west coast and Alaska. Like the highway, the airfield would be part of a western defence system recommended by the Joint Canadian-American Defence Board.

Preliminary surveys, conducted at both Smithers and Telkwa, favored an area adjacent to Lake Kathlyn. In fact, those surveys indicated soil formation and drainage at Lake Kathlyn were even more favourable than conditions encountered at the Prince George Airport.

By August 1941 the final decision had been made and eight men were employed clearing land for a 4,400 foot runway with a paved width of 150 feet. Two months later work began on the administration building and residences. Work on the actual airfield was completed in 1942 as was

The Smithers Airport.

Employee residences on the Smithers Airport.

Although Smithers was far from any major battlefields, there were signs of military activity in the area. With the threat of the Japanese off the west coast, the 14th Aerodrome Defence Company was dispatched to Smithers to protect the upgraded airport. The 50-man Company was in Smithers from January to May 1943, and was then transferred to Annette Island in Alaska.

installation of a 24-hour-a-day radio beam service for aircraft flying in bad weather or at night. The radio range station was constructed just west of the experimental farm and can still be seen today.

Smithers also felt the war in terms of those who risked and, in some cases, sacrificed their lives. By November, 1941, a nationwide conscription program was in effect requiring all males 16 years and over to register for military duty. A year later all females between the ages of 20 and 24 were also required to register.

Late in 1943 The Interior News provided this list of "Bulkley Valley boys who have enlisted" in The Armed Forces.

Henry Anderson
William Apps
Joe Aida
Frank Barker
John Barker

Carl Anderson
Des Agnew
William Beaton
George Bowie
Arthur Berg

Ernie Bodger
Chas. Botham
Doug Bamford
Joe Cunliffe
Wm. Collison
Graham Collison
Ken Collison
Bob Clark (Forestdale)
Fred Chuprun
John Dunlop
Jorgen Dahlie
A.N. Dando
George Durham
Fred Evitt
J.H. Ekman
Cliff Emerson
Bud Gazely
Ed Grant
Gordon Hetherington
A.H. Howells
George Hibbs
Bill Hann
Clive Hoskins
John Johnson
Phillip Kenney
Mel Kerr
Norm Kilpatrick
Grover Loveless
Guy Ludgate
Buck Morris
Craig Millar
Dan Middleton
Lawrence Murray
David MacBean
Jack McDonnell
Stan Noble
Sam Nutter
Dan Palumbo
Harry Quick
Vic Ross
Frank Simmonds
James Seeley
Bob Stephens
Don Sutherland
Fred Tanner
L.N. Warner
Robert Westle
David Oland
Irvine Wade
James J. Wilkinson Sr.
Vimy Windt
Gordon Williams

Bruce Bateson
Wm. F. Burmeister
Alfred Bamford
Ray Cunliffe
Don Collison
Tom Collison
Jack Chapman
Fred Castell (Evelyn)
Pat Downey
Chris Dahlie
Halvor Dahlie
Charlie Doodson
Cec Ebert
R.D. Evans
Armour Emerson
J.H. (Jiggs) Graham
Fred Giraud
Tom Hetherington
Stan Heavysides
Bill Hewson
Harry Haftner
Ed Harding Jr.
Ben Hug
Tom Jones
Doug Kerr
Larry Kemple
Billy Leach
Bob Laidlaw
Arthur Martin
Pete Mayer
Isaac Middleton
Harry Monkley
Wm. McMillan
Dick MacDonald
Mel McIntyre
Alistair McKinnon
Mike O'Neill
Bud Ponder
Garnet Quick
Allan McGill
Alfred Seeley
Frank Smith
Walter Syrnyk
Harold Tanner
Norm Tycho
Wm. Westle
Fred Watson
Walter Watson
John Williams
Bud Washbern
James J. Wilkinson Jr.
Harold Windt
John Yelich

The list is by no means complete but does give an indication of the kind of participation forthcoming from an area of comparatively few souls. Stories were numerous in the war year papers of coincidental meetings between Bulkley Valley soldiers in Europe as were reports of men either killed or missing in action.

Typical of such reports was the following carried in the August 2, 1944 edition of The Interior News.

"Word was received yesterday afternoon by Mrs. Fred Watson that her son WO2 Frederick S. Watson is reported missing while in action overseas with the R.C.A.F. following air operations on July 29th. The action is presumed to be the 1,000 plane raid on Hamburg on that date.

"Freddie has been overseas since March 1943 and up to July 19 had completed 32 trips over Europe. On two occasions previously the crew had brought their plane, Hell's Angels, back for crash landings, the second resulting in its loss. They had just received a new plane, S for Sugar, and it was in this plane that they are reported missing.

"Freddie transferred to Air Force Training early in May, 1942, after serving a few months in the army, and received his navigators wings shortly before going overseas."

For all of those who died during World War II, a Civic Centre Memorial Association was formed in 1945 with Oswald Hoskins as chairman. Funds were to be raised by the association to build a new civic centre that would commemorate the "services and sacrifices of our young people." The early efforts of this association eventually culminated in construction of the existing Smithers Civic Centre, completed during the late 1950's.

Things progressed a bit more quickly in connection with what was, up until 1966, another of Smithers' landmarks. In March of 1943 a decision was taken to replace the original 1914 Bulkley River bridge at the foot of Main Street. The new bridge was to be 534 feet long, 16 feet wide and supported by four piers, two at either shore and two in the river. The actual deck of the new bridge was to be constructed "3½ feet higher than the old one," according to The Interior News, "to provide additional clearance from ice jams and high water."

Unfortunately, not even that precaution was sufficient. On Easter Sunday, 1966, an ice jam on the river broke, sending a wall of ice and water slamming into the side of the structure. A motorist two-thirds of the way across the bridge when it was hit managed to back off the span as the third pier collapsed. Harry Kruisselbrink, one of the first people on the scene, said the motorist stood ashen-faced beside his car as he watched the bridge collapse in front of him. "He would surely have been killed if he hadn't immediately backed off," Kruisselbrink said. Residents living on the east side of the river were ferried back and forth by helicopter (at 50 cents a ride) for the several weeks it took to put a Bailly bridge in place. The Bailly bridge remained in place until the existing bridge, just east of town on Highway 16, was opened for traffic in 1969. The new bridge was part of a re-routing scheme for the highway aimed at reducing the distance between Smithers and Telkwa and eliminating some bad corners.

The Blue Goose Cafe in flames. The Blue Goose was located in the vicinity of the present Northern Star Cafe on Main Street.

The power of the Bulkley was, however, well known prior to the 1966 washout. In fact, at one point early in 1945, the Smithers Chamber of Commerce was seriously encouraging dam construction on the river. Members present at the January 15 meeting "were unanimous in a decision to urge the provincial government to look into the feasibility of developing the hydro-electric possibilities of the Bulkley River as a cheap source of power for the Bulkley Valley." Victoria, fortunately, acted with the same urgency on this request as it had on the federal government's suggestion of financial help for the Prince Rupert to Hazelton leg of Highway 16.

The mid-1940's in Smithers saw two of the community's worst fires. The first, on May 6, 1944, started about 9 p.m. in the Blue Goose Cafe on Main Street. By the time the blaze had been brought under control Anger's Tailor Shop, the Noel Dry Goods and Furniture Store, the Day Bakery in the Newbery Building and the former Gray Jewelry Store (then vacant) had all been destroyed. The McRae Hotel on Broadway Avenue was damaged, as were Eby's Hardware, the Hanson Co. building, the Kenney Real Estate office and the Hudson Hotel. The loss was estimated at about $75,000.

Almost a year later, in April 1945, another fire broke out in the same area, this time on Broadway

The Smithers Fire Department — an essential service. Unfortunately, a photo of the fire department in the 40's was not available. This photo was taken in the mid 1950's: L-R: Harry Haywood (fire chief), Bob Williams, Tom Robinson, Toddy Kennedy, Bill Martin, Ed Malkow, Bob Fowler, Bob McEwen, Ed Hinchliffe, Orland Nockelby, Scotty Urquhart, Jack Ekman, Geoff Beley, Arn Van Lieshout, Ray Clarkston, Bonne Koopmans, Don Herman, Oakley McCammon, Bill Jackson, Dick Maywood, Dick Davies, Fred Riffel, Walter Watson, Dan Hawe.

The railway continued to be an important part of Smithers' economy. As time went on, the older employees retired. This is C.N.R. engineer Bill Bayler's last run, circa 1940's: L-R: Jim Kelly, Frank Foster, Roy Cheater, Stan Jones, Percy Emerson, George Raymond, Mrs. Bayler, Bob Davidson, Bill Bayler, H.M. Triplett (chief dispatcher), Frank Parker, Bill Fisher, Dick Champion, Jim Buchan, Pete Berg and Jim Silver.

just off Main Street. A total of eight buildings were destroyed, including Elliot's Shoe Store, the Kennedy Building, which housed the OK Cafe, Walls Garage, Stewarts Cafe, the rebuilt Day Bakery and the Bowland Building. The loss was estimated at more than $100,000.

Other major events which marked the decade of the 1940's included the advent of long distance telephone service in July, 1946, and a referendum in which village residents gave their approval for the community's first water system. The vote, taken on July 29, 1947, was reported by The Interior News as follows.

> "Taxpayers of the community emphatically endorsed the proposal of the Village Commissioners to borrow $106,000 for the construction of a water system when they went to the polls on Saturday. Voting on the by-law went 164 in favor, 52 against, and 9 ballots spoiled."

Later that year, in December, the man who had actually been awarded the contract by the G.T.P. to clear the townsite back in 1913, opened his new garage at the corner of Main and Third Avenue. W.J. (Wiggs) O'Neill's new premises marked the G.M dealer's second expansion since initially opening his car business in 1919.

O'Neill, who died in 1964 at the age of 82, was

W.J. "Wiggs" O'Neill, entrepeneur, local historian and colorful character.

A typical bush sawmill. Mills like this once formed a major part of the local economy and provided much employment.

Another bush mill.

Skidding logs the old fashioned way — with horses.

Gordon Jewell of Northern Interior Forest Products Ltd.

Miller's sawmill in the 40's. L-R: Harry Haywood and Ben Miller (owner of the mill).

born in the gold rush town of Barkerville, later moving with his family to the Queen Charlotte Islands and then to Port Simpson where he grew up.

During the construction of the G.T.P., he operated stern wheel steamers on the Skeena and Bulkley Rivers, hauling freight and passengers to the head of the steel. Later, he operated a Packard truck carrying supplies and people between Hazelton and Aldermere. After overseeing the clearing of the Smithers townsite in 1913, he built a garage, theatre and electric light plant in the new community.

A General Motors dealer here for 47 years, Wiggs also found time to record his colorful history and that of the area in three books entitled "Steamboat Days on the Skeena", "Whitewater Men" and "Along The Totem Trail."

Another batch of 2x4's coming up! Harry Bakker at the controls.

"Home, Sweet Home" for bush mill employees. As can be imagined, bush cabins of yesteryear lacked some of the modern conveniences now considered essential.

The 1940's also saw the emergence of the independent sawmill operator. According to Ralph Dieter, who operated three different mills himself at various times, the industry really began to flourish with the end of the war in 1945.

"There were hundreds of them in the valley, all independents, and many of them had farming operations, too" he said. "There were half a dozen in the Driftwood area alone . . . myself, Bill Morris, Bill Hinchliffe, the Lubbers brothers from Telkwa, Dick Gilbert, Hans Tugnum."

Pete Dieleman's sawmill on Dennis Lake, one of the larger bush mills. This operation eventually evolved into the D.Groot Logging Ltd. complex on Tatlow Road.

Timber, according to Ralph, was easy to get in those days.

"You just had to apply for it . . . 15 to 20 acres up to a quarter section. Then you'd order a mill from Vancouver, Edmonton or Calgary and get to work."

Trees were cut with power saws, somewhat cruder versions than those available today, and then drawn to the actual mill site by horse. A typical operation would involve about six people, including one or two fallers, a sawyer, and an edgerman. A small mill could produce from 2,000 to 4,000 feet daily while the larger operations could turn out 10,000 feet of rough lumber.

The rough lumber would then be transported to a local buyer, such as Gordon Jewell of Northern Interior Forest Products in Smithers, who would run it through his planer mill before shipping it out.

According to Ralph, the independent operator had about 10 good years before falling out of favor with the B.C. Forest Service.

"It was too much of a problem for them to watch us all," he said. "In fact, a cruiser for forestry once told me I wouldn't be getting any more sales because the forest service was going to eliminate the small operators."

The first step in the eventual demise of the independents was the establishment of a quota system, limiting the amount of timber available to each operator. Their numbers gradually decreased until, in 1970, a very large and up-to-date mill, now Northwood, was established in Houston. The owners bought up all the quotas held by the Independents and their mills, according to Ralph.

'They spent millions just buying people out. They'd offer almost anything to get rid of you.''

The planned demise of the valley's independent sawmill operations represented the end of an era, as had the gradual decline of tie hacking operations. But both during and after the war the community continued to experience the loss of its links with another, earlier era. Fate and the simple passage of time was gradually removing those who represented the area's beginnings and another way of life.

One such person was Ben Nelson who used to live on the site of what is now the King residence on Driftwood Road. He disappeared early in the decade, the event being recorded in the following way by the local newspaper.

''Provincial police have so far failed to unravel the mystery of the disappearance of Ben Nelson, prospector and packer, of this district, who left here last summer in company with Joe Murray and Ralph Dieter on a prospecting trip to Chuckachida Lake, north of Hazelton. The expedition broke up however when first Dieter and then Murray abandoned it, leaving Nelson to go on alone.

''Since that occasion little had been heard of Ben until police were informed by P.M. Monckton that he had seen the lone traveller at the head of the Klappan River and that the latter had told him of seeing Ed Borders and had asked him to get in touch with Murray at Thistles Mine, Port Alberni, to arrange for a plane to fly provisions to Chuckachida Lake.

''The possibility that Ben may be stranded in the north without provisions was seen by a message received by police stating that Indians had found a message on April 30th, on a cabin door at Spatsizi near the Ducker River, signed by Nelson and saying that he

Law and order, a necessity in any community. Shown here are: Front (L-R): Harvey Davies, magistrate, Jim Kirby, retired B.C. Provincial policeman, Ken McRae, Government Agent. Rear: B.C. Provincial police staff Corporal Zorn, Sgt. Brunton, Stacey Davies and Ed Corsons.

Jim Kirby, retired B.C. Provincial policeman, who spearheaded the famous chase for Simon Gunanoot in Hazelton. Kirby reached his 100th birthday in 1964. He is presented with a plaque commemorating the occasion by the Rotary Club President Gerry Brinkman.

Ben Nelson, packer, in front of his cabin, 1938. Bill Davidson photo.

R.S. "Dick" Sargent.

had lost all his provisions and clothing. The Indians later found his overturned raft."

Nelson's remains were found that summer (1941) in the Chuckachida Lake area. Indications were that without provisions, the hardships of the northern winter proved too great and he had starved to death.

That same year the community learned of the death of Rev. F.L. Stephenson, the first minister to serve both Telkwa and Smithers. Rev. Stephenson, who was 76 when he died, arrived in the valley during the century's first decade having driven his dog team south from Atlin.

In July, 1941, Wiggs O'Neill acted as master of ceremonies for a party honoring the 50th anniversary of Richard S. (Dick) Sargent's arrival in Hazelton. Smithers village clerk J.W. (Happy) Turner, by then a 33-year resident of the valley himself, and Telkwa oldtimer Frank Dockrill also attended the event. Sargent, pioneer merchant of Hazelton during the 1890's, also operated stores in Telkwa and Smithers during his lengthy business career. He died three years after the anniversary celebration in August, 1944.

Closer to home, Smithers residents joined Mr. and Mrs. John S. Gray in celebrating their 50th wedding anniversary in December, 1941. The Grays were both born in Scotland, married December 4, 1891, and came to Canada in 1898, settling first in Montreal. They arrived in Smithers in 1913. Gray, in addition to operating his own jewelry store, also served as watch inspector for the C.N.R. and founded the first Smithers Band. He died about eight months after his golden wedding anniversary on September 29, 1942.

Another of the valley's oldest residents died three months later in December. Wm. Croteau, born 1869 in Levis, Que., arrived in the valley in 1906, settling just east of what was then Aldermere. He served briefly as a real estate agent in

Happy Turner and Jim Kennedy, circa 1955. Turner was Village Clerk for many years and Kennedy was proprietor of Kennedy's poolroom.

the area and later as secretary of the Bulkley Valley Farmers Institute.

In 1943, death claimed Father Nicholas Coccola, resident chaplain at the Bulkley Valley District Hospital for nine years, H.B. Campbell, who had succeeded Stephen H. Hoskins as government agent in 1931, and A.T. Harrer, former Smithers mill owner and long time valley prospector.

Two other members of the valley's earliest mining fraternity also passed away during the 40's. Charles Gordon (Peavine) Harvey died August 31, 1945 at the age of 90, the victim of a heart attack. As testimony to his endurance, Peavine had taken out his 56th free miner's licence two years previously, having staked his first claim in 1887.

A couple of years later Peavine's colleague, Joseph (Kicker) Kelly, also passed away. He was 79. An excerpt from his obituary stated:

> "Joe's views on politics and world events were offered freely to anyone who would listen and his arguments on current topics, if not any too convincing, were backed by the courage of his own convictions."

Before the end of the decade Smithers was to lose three more of its pioneers. Dr. H.C. Hankinson, then living in Prince Rupert, and Charlie Morris, local butcher, impromptu hospital chef during the 1918 influenza epidemic and Smithers mayor for one year, both died in June 1949. In September E.E. Orchard, the village's second mayor, died at his home in Bremerton, Washington.

Smithers was, however, to continue the tradition of growth so firmly established by these

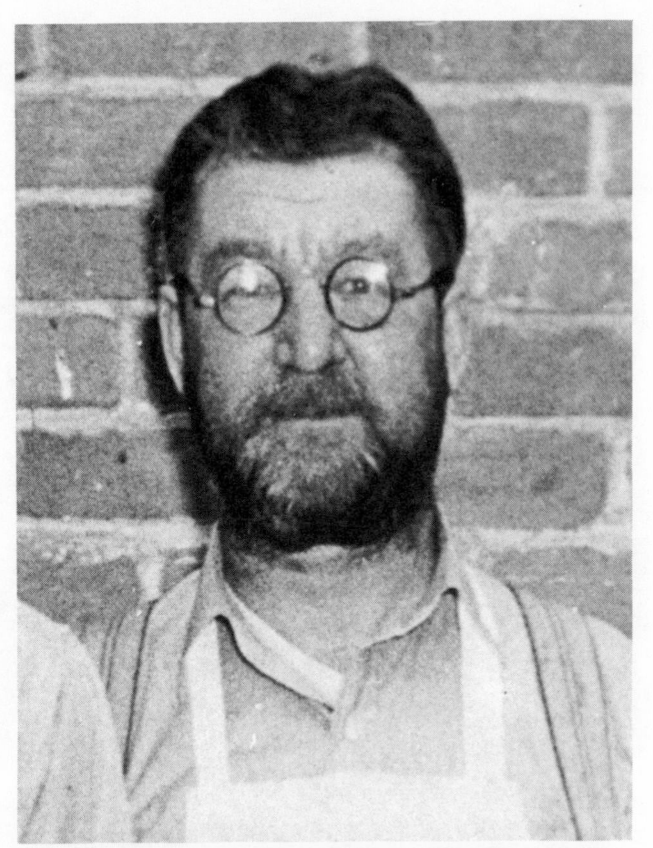

C.E. "Charlie" Morris, Chairman of the Village Commissioners, 1942.

original community architects. Never was this more in evidence than on the eve of 1950. Work was already underway on a new covered curling rink on First Avenue, two blocks west of Main Street. A new nurses residence, which continues to serve the community today, was opened adjacent to the hospital on May 21, 1949. On December 29, 1949, the federal government announced it had purchased the old Elks Hall site, at Main and Second, for construction of a new federal building. A sum of $50,000 was set aside for construction of the building which was to house the community post office. In addition work was started on a new road that was to run from Sealy's corner to Babine Lake.

Nineteen forty-nine was also the year in which the Aluminum Company of Canada undertook studies into the hydro-electric potential of the Ootsa Lake area. Although the actual damming of the Nechako River, the construction of the Kemano power plant and establishment of the Kitimat aluminum smelter were still in the future, the decision to proceed was never really in doubt. As one Alcan vice-president said at the time:

> ". . . the co-operative attitude of the government leaders and the energy and initiative in support of the project shown by Lands Minister (E.T.) Kenney have gone a long way

The social event of the year — Klondike Days, 1949. The Elks Hall, located where the Post Office now stands, was transformed into the "Dirty Shame Saloon" for the occasion.

Moricetown's contribution to Klondike Days: L-R: Charley Tommie, George Naziel, David Dennis, Alex Tiljoe, Jack Joseph, Jimmy Morris and Jimmy Michell.

in encouraging the company to go ahead with the second phase of its engineering work."

The dam eventually erected on the Nechako River was fittingly named after the project's most ardent supporter, The Hon. E.T. Kenney, M.L.A. for Skeena.

As the decade drew to a close there were promises afoot of other major developments that would change the character of the community. Rural electrification was a regular topic of discussion. According to officials of the B.C. Power Commission, there were 71 potential customers in the Driftwood area requiring an estimated 34 miles of distribution line. The provision of power to the Evelyn and Round Lake areas was also being studied at this time. In addition the town was discussing a plan to lay ashphalt on Main Street for the first time since the street's construction 36 years before and government officals were suggesting the paving of Highway 16 could begin sometime in 1950.

The 1940's had been a significant decade in Smithers' evolution. Creation of the road link to the west coast and establishment of the airport further enhanced the community's access to southern and eastern market places. By the same token, however, Smithers was now more prone to the pressures of financial and social conformity powerfully exerted by the people and institutions of larger urban centres in the province and the nation. If the community had developed any strength of character, any sense of unique identity, those traits were now to be tested.

The new Federal Building under construction, 1953-54. It houses the Post Office on its main floor and is probably the most popular building in town, outdrawing even that other popular government institution — the liquor store.

E.T. Kenney.

The Fall Fair parade down Main Street, August 27, 1949. Main Street was not paved until 1952.

Inaugural meeting of the Smithers Junior Chamber of Commerce, 1949. The gathering included many unidentified guests. Among the Smithers members present were: Gordon Williams, Tat Aida, Hartley Fawcett, Wilson Muirhead, Nick Picul, Walter Burns, Stan Gould, Bill Leach, Keith Elliot, Ben Hug, Jorgen Dahlie, Larry White, Jack Chapman, Pat Carr, Gordon Hetherington, Bob McEwen, Ken Warner, Bill Grey, Cliff Emerson, Owen Hooper, Ian Panton, Bob Clarke, Dave Roumieu, Ted Chapman, Stacey Davies, Cliff DeGrasse, Wells Herriett, Len Evans, Bill Bovill, Harry Haywood, Fred Riffel and Walter Watson.

Smithers in the 1940's.

Picture Scrapbook

HARDWARE

G.C.K.
Dance for Canadian Patriotic Fund
Smithers B.C.

Bulkley Valley Wildlife

Hudson Bay Mountain and Lake Kathlyn — a peaceful scene and an indication why people came to the Valley — and stayed. B.C. Government photo.

EPILOGUE

By 1950 the building blocks were firmly in place. The Smithers of the future would depend heavily for its livelihood on lumber, the railroad, agriculture and an aggressive business community. In this last area of endeavour much of the activity was already in the hands of second generation Smithereens. Ken Warner was now in charge of the newspaper. Oswald Hoskins had a prospering car dealership while the Goodacres were firming up their grip on the grocery business. Wilfred Watson had taken over as manager of the Hudson Hotel, built by his father Fred, and the

The Hudson Hotel. B.C. Provincial Archives photo.

The 1950's were the era of immigrant arrivals in the Bulkley Valley, many of them Dutch and Italian. Some of the Italian immigrants at a christening conducted by Father John Callaly (centre). L-R: William Mellace, Gioconda Mellace, Ted Mellace, Rosa Mellace, Frank Cuglietta, Anna Pullano, Maria Mellace. The baby is Anna Cuglietta.

Dutch immigrants at a triple wedding. At the front table, L-R: Francis and Alice Stam, Nick and Sophia DeWitt, John and Cecile Konst. Among the guests: Tina Mulder, Mr. and Mrs. Frits Buursema, Mr. and Mrs. Theo Bandstra, Mr. and Mrs. John Bandstra, Mrs. Bill Vandergrift, Bert Haar, Pete Dieleman, and Mr. and Mrs. A. Konst.

O'Neill brothers were preparing to take over from their father at Smithers Garage.

There was still talk, as there had been since the town's earliest days, of a major population influx and business expansion, although no one was now predicting Smithers would become the Spokane of the North. Indeed there were significant additions to the population which began after World War II and continued through the 1950's. During these years a number of immigrant families relocated here, adding greatly to the cultural diversity but occasioning no overnight growth in the tax rolls.

There were, of course, notable spurts of expansion; the civic centre, new schools, the new government building on Alfred Avenue, a shopping mall, two large sawmills and the new curling rink to list a few. But these additions seemed the natural consequence of changing market conditions and an annual four per cent growth rate in the population. There was really very little variation in the pattern during the three decades from 1950.

Then, during late 1979, Smithers began to experience a period of growth not seen since the original town site construction during 1913-14. Government offices were being relocated here, the geographical centre of the district, creating a shortage of office space. Tourism had caught up to and surpassed available accommodation. A refurbished Main Street was beginning to attract more and more retail trade. All of these things gave way to a building boom about mid-1980 involving new hotels, apartment buildings, office space, retail stores and private homes. After more than 65 years, two wars and a depression, the dream of a major community expansion was finally being experienced. The long term implications of this rapid growth remain a matter of some discussion. Nonetheless, on the eve of Smithers' official 60th birthday, the local economy had never looked brighter.

Friesen
Printers
announces its
"Family History"
program.
We can help
you to produce
your family's
history.
Write to:
Friesen Printers
Box 720
Altona, Manitoba
R0G 0B0

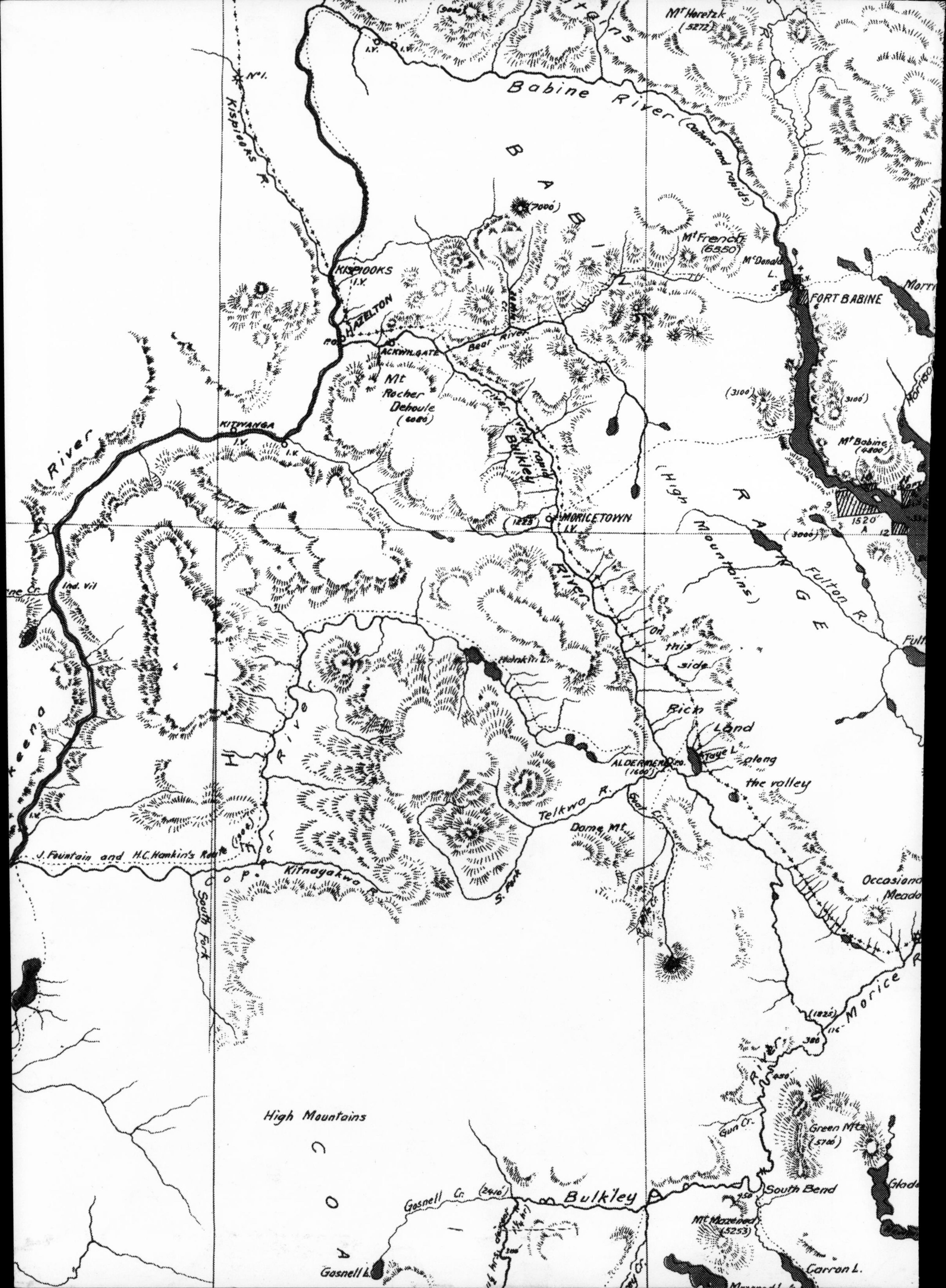

Mt Horetzk (5272)
Babine River (Cañons and rapids)
BABINE RANGE
(7000')
Mt French (6550)
McDonald L.
FORT BABINE
Kispiooks R.
KISPIOOKS I.V.
HAZELTON
ACKWILGATE
Bear River
Mt Rocher Deboule (6080)
KITWANGA I.V.
River
(3100')
Mt Babine (4800)
(High Mountains)
MORICETOWN I.V.
1520
(3000')
Fulton R.
Ind. Vil
Rich Land along the valley
On this side
ALDERMERE P.O. (1600')
Telkwa R.
Dome Mt.
J. Fountain and H.C. Hankin's Route
Kitnagakwa R.
S. Fork
South Fork
Occasional Meadows
Morice R.
(1825)
Morice River
Gun Cr.
Green Mts (5700)
High Mountains
Gosnell Cr.
(2410')
Bulkley
South Bend
Mt Mazened (5253)
Gosnell L.
Carron L.